Just a Scrap of Paper

KURT JOHNSON

Life-Changing
Stories From
the Voice of Prophecy
Bible School

Just a Scrap of Paper

Pacific Press®
Publishing Association

Nampa, Idaho | Oshawa, Ontario, Canada
www.pacificpress.com

Cover design by Steve Lanto
Cover design resources from iStockphoto.com
Inside design by Kristin Hansen-Mellish

You can obtain additional copies of this book by calling toll-free
1-800-765-6955 or by visiting http://www.adventistbookcenter.com.

The authors assume full responsibility for the accuracy of all facts and
quotations as cited in this book.

Library of Congress Cataloging-in-Publication Data:

Johnson, Kurt W., 1950–
   Just a scrap of paper : Life-changing stories from the Voice of Prophecy
Bible School / Kurt W. Johnson.
      p. cm.
   ISBN 13: 978-0-8163-4515-1 (pbk.)
   ISBN 10: 0-8163-4515-5 (pbk.)
   1. Voice of Prophecy Bible School—Anecdotes. 2. Bible—Study and
teaching—Seventh-day Adventists—Anecdotes. I. Title.
   BS603.J64 2013
   220.071'073—dc23
                                                   2013003445

13 14 15 16 17 • 5 4 3 2 1

Contents

Introduction

The Oldest Continuous Christian Radio Bible Correspondence School

The *Voice of Prophecy* radio broadcast was a pioneer of media ministry in the Seventh-day Adventist Church and is one of the oldest continuous Christian radio broadcasts in North America. As this book is written, the ministry is eighty-four years old, and the Bible correspondence school just completed its seventieth year. To my knowledge it is the oldest radio Bible correspondence school of any denomination.

The Voice of Prophecy Bible Correspondence School in North America is the mother of all the Bible correspondence schools operated by the Seventh-day Adventist Church around the world. Just one year following the birth of the Bible school in North America, a similar school was launched in Central and South America in both the Spanish and Portuguese languages. Today, there are Bible schools and affiliates in some 140 countries worldwide. Millions of individuals have graduated from these schools over the past seventy years. It is truly remarkable what God has done!

Today, the Internet and other new technologies have joined with the printed Bible study guides to bring biblical truth to the current generation. In addition, the Voice of Prophecy Bible School is a team ministry, working with numerous other media ministries and publishing ministries of the Seventh-day Adventist Church.

To mark the seventieth anniversary of the Voice of Prophecy Bible School, I've prepared this book to tell its story—and the stories of some of those who have found God's message of truth and hope through its ministry. These are reminders of what God has done through the Bible study guides and dedicated church members to influence scores of people for eternity. As you read these stories of changed lives, may God be glorified through our acknowledging the great things He has done!

Kurt W. Johnson
Bible School Director
Voice of Prophecy

A Broken Leg, a Radio Broadcast, and a Bible Lesson

Russell Burrill

It's because of a broken leg caused "by those annoying Adventists," that I am one of them today!

My New England roots go deep. I grew up in northeastern Massachusetts, where my family has lived for nearly four hundred years. In fact, some of my ancestors arrived in 1620 on the *Mayflower.* The Burrill family were faithful Baptists and attended church every Sunday.

Early in my life, I sensed a call to ministry and decided as a young teenager to become a Baptist minister. I had never heard of Seventh-day Adventists and wasn't aware there was a small Adventist church of twenty-five members in my hometown—population 50,000. Another town, ten miles away, had no Adventist church although it had a population of 100,000. So this one small Adventist church in my hometown served 150,000 people. Little wonder I was not aware of it.

At the age of fourteen I was teaching a class of nine- to twelve-year-olds every Sunday and was actively involved in all the church activities for young people. About this time I got one of my first jobs—a paper route. And this is where the story becomes interesting.

My paper route led to my first contact with Seventh-day Adventists. Three of my customers were Adventists. This was strange, because the Adventist church was across the river on the other side of town and had very few members. I learned quickly about Adventists; I learned they were my worst customers! Collection night was Friday evening, and they wouldn't pay me if I showed up after sundown. I had to come back to collect at another time.

One Friday evening, when I was a freshman in high school, the sky was sporting colors of orange, yellow, and purple as the sun dropped below the horizon. I was nearing the end of my paper delivery route and was only one door away from one of my Adventist customers. If I hurried, I could get there before sundown and collect payment that Friday; if I was later, I'd have to come back another time. Finishing the collection at the house next door as quickly as I could, I raced down the steps and onto the icy sidewalk. Immediately, my legs flew into the air, and I came crashing down on the concrete, breaking my right leg in two places—all because of those "stupid Adventists!"

For me, the worst part was being confined to bed for the next three months. Because I couldn't climb the stairs to my bedroom, my bed was set up in the living room. There I could watch TV and interact with the family. I never went back to school that year. I wasn't able to walk, even using crutches, until the middle of June. So I had to finish my freshman year of high school by correspondence.

My biggest regret was that I couldn't go to church or Sunday School to teach my class. Thus, when my parents and brother left for church, I contented myself by listening to religious programs on the radio.

One particular Sunday morning, I heard a new program that began with a quartet singing "Lift up the trumpet; and loud let it ring!" I listened intently as the speaker, H. M. S. Richards Sr., opened the Word of God and explained it. Then the program offered a Bible course by correspondence. Because I had little else to do, I enrolled in the Faith Bible Course, the adult course at the time, consisting of forty lessons. I thought that taking this course would be excellent preparation for becoming a Baptist minister. Little did I know that the correspondence course was connected to the very people who had caused me to break my leg! I did not discover this fact, however, until I studied the lesson on the topic of the Sabbath. God works in mysterious ways!

I continued the lessons. Because I had all the time in the world lying flat on my back, I finished the entire course in three months. After I completed the Faith course, the pastor of the local Adventist church visited me and invited me to attend his church. Because he had visited me, I felt obligated to attend—once! Can you imagine what happened next? The Adventist pastor arranged for someone to pick me up and bring me to church—and it was the same people who lived in the house I was going to collect from when I fell and broke my leg! How ironic! That first visit to the little Adventist church was not my last. This began a strange journey for me—going to church on Saturday afternoons.

By this time, my dad discovered what was going on, and he became greatly upset. Dad was one of those "born a Baptist, going to die a Baptist" kind of people, and he did not want his son mixed up in this strange, new religion. A series of arguments began that lasted for the next two or three years.

My dad was very active in the Baptist church and a personal friend of the pastor. This particular Baptist church was the church in which my dad had grown up and where my parents were married. Now that family legacy was being threatened by my desire to keep the Sabbath.

We lived just twenty miles from the Atlantic Ocean. One of my favorite foods during my childhood was fried clams. Of course, my dad knew this, and he also knew what I had learned from Leviticus—about not eating unclean foods. On a family outing to the ocean we followed our regular tradition: stopping for fried clams. My dad dangled them in front of my nose, trying to tempt me, but I was able to resist. In addition, when I had first decided to no longer eat unclean foods, my mother served ham for lunch. I didn't eat lunch that day. At supper I was famished—and she served leftover ham! It was a very difficult time for a growing teenager concerned about following the Bible.

With my ever-increasing interest in Adventism, my dad decided he needed to get me away from Massachusetts. He packed up our family and moved us to Florida, simply to get away from the Adventists. Little did he realize there were more Adventists in Florida than in Massachusetts!

After arriving in Florida, Dad immediately began searching for a Baptist church for the family to attend. He didn't realize that the Baptists in Florida were Southern Baptists and very different from the American Baptist denomination that we belonged to in Massachusetts. So he was finding it extremely difficult to locate the right church. After some persuasion, I was able to get my mother to attend the Adventist church with me. Our attendance lasted three weeks and created such a storm of arguments at home that we were unable to go back. Only Dad drove, and he refused to take us, and we knew no Adventists who could pick us up.

During a six-month period in Florida, Dad moved our family three times, trying to find an acceptable Baptist church, but nothing worked out. So, after six months, we moved back to Massachusetts. Dad was hoping that if we got back into our previous Baptist church, we would all be happy again.

We arrived back home to a bombshell—the pastor, whom my dad loved, had had an affair with one of the members and was being dismissed. The news devastated Dad. He never went back to the Baptist church. By this time, I was discouraged as well, and as a result no one in our family went to any church!

However by the fall of 1957, I made a decision to begin keeping the Sabbath. I was sixteen now and able to drive. I was looking for a part-time job, and when I interviewed I would announce that I was a Seventh-day Adventist and could not work from sundown Friday to sundown Saturday. (At the time I wasn't even attending the Adventist Church.) Amazingly, I was hired at a local convenience store with the understanding that I wouldn't work on Sabbath. The next Sabbath I was in church, and Mom and my brother quickly joined me. Even Dad relented and actually drove us to church!

Every Saturday Dad would drive my mother, my brother, and me to the Adventist church. While we attended Sabbath School and the worship service, he would go to the library and search for ammunition to prove that the Adventist theology was wrong. One Sabbath when he picked us up from his library excursion, he was bursting at the seams with news. "Guess what?" he shouted. "I found out 'those Advents' [this was his name for Adventists] wash each other's feet in church!" We assured him that we had attended now for several months and nothing like that had ever happened. Well, the very next Sabbath was Communion Sabbath, and Dad was correct. "Those Advents" did wash each other's feet!

For two years, every Sabbath was a confrontation over our church attendance. But, every Sabbath we would attend, and Dad would head to the library. The Adventist pastor, consistently visited us in our home. But as soon as my dad saw his car in the driveway, he would go to the basement and work on the boat he was building. The Adventist pastor was smart. As soon as he finished visiting with my mom, my brother, and me, he immediately opened the basement door—without asking—and went down to visit my dad. The pastor never talked religion; he showed an interest in Dad and his projects. He learned that my dad liked to fish; so he offered to go fishing with him. Dad couldn't resist that. Hence, he and the Adventist pastor went fishing together and started building a relationship. Dad never understood why the Adventist pastor always insisted that Dad keep all the fish, but he enjoyed the companionship.

On a January Sabbath morning in 1958, we were waiting for Dad to come out of the bedroom and take us to church. To our shock, he came out dressed in his suit and declared that he was going to find out about "those Advents" firsthand. He never missed another Sabbath! Dad was born a Baptist, but died an Adventist colporteur.

In October 1958, after my entire family had been attending the Adventist church for more than nine months, the new Baptist preacher came to visit us. I was the only one at home when he arrived. I begin to shower him with questions about the Sabbath. He became extremely frustrated when he couldn't answer my questions.

I worked each evening, and the pastor decided to come back when I wasn't home. One night I arrived home from work and learned that the Baptist pastor had visited and had become quite vehement in his denunciation of Adventists, calling them every name in the book. He infuriated my dad so much that even before I came home that night, Dad had already called the Adventist pastor to tell him that all of us wanted to be baptized the next Sabbath!

On November 1, 1958, the four of us were led into the waters of baptism, recommitting our lives to Christ and becoming members of the Seventh-day Adventist Church. We had never been given Bible studies. We had never attended an Adventist evangelistic meeting. Our contact was primarily through the radio ministry and Bible School of the Voice of Prophecy, "a voice crying in the wilderness" that reached our hearts. Without this ministry we might never have become Seventh-day Adventists. We thank God for what the Voice of Prophecy did in helping us to become a part of this church with a special message for the last days.

℃∕⊃

Russell Burrill, DMin, has served as pastor, evangelist, seminary professor, and several positions in the NAD, including director of the North American Division Evangelism Institute (Andrews University). Russell and his wife, Cynthia, have two children.

What God Do You Serve?

Michael L. Ryan

I was deep in northern India in a small room that was crowded with eighteen people. Bold praise to God fell upon eager ears. The pastor testified how the veil of fear had been lifted and evil spirits banished. A new congregation now worshiped the true and living God.

Wrapped in a tattered brown blanket, an old man sat quietly listening. I looked at him carefully. A white paper clip connected the earpiece of his glasses to the frame. The lenses were thick and foggy. There was a small hole in the collar of his shirt. Clearly, he was not numbered among the earth's wealthy people. Yet, an electric smile found its way through well-established wrinkles. Occasionally, he wiped tears from his eyes with a small, white cloth.

"He is my assistant," the pastor said, breaking into my thoughts.

"He is your assistant?" I blurted, involuntarily betraying my surprise.

At that, the old man began to speak softly. His story went something like this:

"In 1954," he said, "I had a job sweeping out the train station. One day, in a pile of trash, I came across a little card. I could read enough to determine that it was an invitation to study the Bible. I kept the card for several days and then decided to try to learn what Christians believed. I mailed the card to an address in Pune, India. When the first lesson arrived, I discovered I needed a Bible. It took me four months to save enough money to buy a Bible. Because I read so poorly, it took me three more months to complete and return the first lesson. I struggled to complete the eight introductory lessons. Eighteen months had passed since I found the card.

"I then requested the advanced course of thirty-six lessons. Lesson by lesson, my reading was improving, but finding postage money was a challenge. It took me three and a half years to complete the advanced course. In 1959, I received a certificate of graduation.

"Armed with my Bible, I set out to find other Christians. I couldn't find any Christians anywhere. Finally, in 1967, a new Christian group was formed in my area. I began worshiping with them, but after two years they asked me not to return, because my beliefs differed from theirs. I found another Christian group that had just started, but soon this group also asked me to leave because of doctrinal differences. For many years I roamed from group to group, studying the Bible with a small group of friends, always faithfully holding to the truths of the Bible as I had learned them in the lessons.

"In 1994, now an old man, I attended the funeral of a friend. A young man was conducting the service. This young man used the occasion to provide biblical instruction about heaven, the state of the dead, Jesus' second coming, and the resurrection. At the conclusion of the service, I eagerly questioned the young man, because his teachings perfectly matched my own beliefs.

"This young man, thinking I was a Hindu, asked, 'What god do you serve?'

"In all innocence, I replied, 'I worship the God of the Voice of Prophecy.' "

As the old man finished his story, I quickly looked over at Division President Elder Ron Watts, who was also attending this meeting in northern India. Tears were streaming down his face as he said in a voice choked with emotion, "Who else . . . who else has been waiting for forty years while faithfully worshiping the God of the Voice of Prophecy?"

Later I had the privilege of speaking to forty-one pioneer members in the first-established Seventh-day Adventist church in that city. The old man, God's faithful servant, was laid to rest in 1998. He rests, not as those without hope, but with the joy and assurance that the God of the Voice of Prophecy is still faithful.

℘

Michael L. Ryan has served in the Philippines, Far Eastern Division, and the General Conference as Global Mission coordinator, a general field secretary and currently as a general vice president. He is married to Laura Jean Ryan, and they have two children.

God Leads a Little Girl in Maine

Ernestine (Teenie) Finley

I was six months old when our family moved from Portland, Maine, to the little town of Millinocket in the northern part of the state. Ours was not a religious home with Christian values. We attended church occasionally at Christmas and Easter. But religion was certainly not a significant part of our daily lives.

From time to time—usually following a string of drunken episodes involving my stepfather—my mom would put my sister and me on a bus to Morrell, Maine, where our grandparents lived. The atmosphere there was entirely different from my home in Millinocket. Instead of continued arguments and conflict, there was family worship, prayer, and Bible reading. I felt loved and secure at my grandparents' house. I was happy there and at peace.

My grandparents had become Seventh-day Adventists some time earlier. Every morning, after breakfast, we had family worship. As a ten-year-old, I enjoyed the fascinating stories from the Bible that Grandpa read. On Friday we prepared for the Sabbath. Because we did not have running water or electricity in the house, we had to draw all our water from a well out back. I still remember filling the tub for our Friday night baths by letting down a pail on a rope, drawing a bucket full of water, and trying to carry it into the bathroom without spilling it! Grandma cooked extra food on Friday. Grandpa and Grandma explained that the next day we would all be going to what they called "Sabbath School." This was new to me. At home, our typical Saturday routine was attending a movie, with enough money to buy a bag of popcorn. At our house, we spent many Friday nights waiting for my stepfather to come home from the bar. But at our grandparents' house we would gather around the piano and sing hymns! This was my first exposure to what true Christianity was all about. I remember hearing Grandpa praying that "these two little girls who don't have the love of a father" would one day know Jesus' love. Many times I carefully listened as my grandfather prayed that God would touch the lives of my sister and me.

But all too soon my mother would arrive to take my sister and me back to a very different environment. I spent most of the first ten years of my life in extremely challenging circumstances at home. In the one house there was peace and calm; the other could explode into conflict instantaneously. I remember a time my stepfather tipped over the dinner plates, throwing them across the dining room, and turning over the kitchen table. Yet in the midst of all this, God protected me. Surprisingly, I was a happy, radiant child. Somehow God was watching over me—just as Grandpa prayed He would.

When my mother had had enough of my stepfather's rampages, we would pack up and leave. One year I changed schools five times! Imagine my hectic, disrupted life—different homes, different schools, and different friends. One particular time Mom said we were leaving my stepfather for good, but just before we moved, the most amazing experience took place.

As I mentioned previously, Grandpa prayed for my sister and me. But he did more than just pray; he actively worked to bring about some kind of religious influence into our lives. He gave my mother's name to a local Seventh-day Adventist colporteur. This man knocked on our door and sold my mom a set of *Bedtime Stories* for my sister and me. I still have those old, red-covered books! Mom also bought a Bible. The colporteur, Mr. Colburn, then asked my mother if she would like to study the Bible through the Voice of Prophecy. Before she could reply, I said excitedly, "I want to take that Bible course!"

I immediately filled out a card requesting the Bible lessons. Mom and I began studying the Bible at the same time. I studied the junior lessons and was amazed at what I discovered. I learned about Jesus and His soon return, the controversy between good and evil, the Bible Sabbath, and why my grandfather worshiped on Saturday. I also learned about healthful living. I remember telling my mother, "I don't want to eat pork anymore. I want to follow the Bible." I couldn't wait to get those lessons each week.

About that time I learned there was also a *Voice of Prophecy* radio program. I listened eagerly, waiting for the Voice of Prophecy quartet to begin singing "Lift up the trumpet, loud let it ring!" It was thrilling to hear Del Delker sing! As a little child of ten years old, I studied the Voice of Prophecy Bible course and listened to the *Voice of Prophecy* radio broadcast. The sermons by H. M. S. Richards powerfully affected my life.

When the Voice of Prophecy staff put those lessons into the mailbag at the office in California, little did they know that the little girl at 98 Bates Street, Millinocket, Maine, would one day be a Seventh-day Adventist evangelist's wife, serving God around the world. But God knew what was taking place—and what would take place! I would go down to the little post office in our town and literally wait for those lessons to come in the mail. Sometimes, I recall, the instructor would write "Excellent" across the top of my lesson. When that happened, I would be so encouraged and think, *That's really good!* It was so exciting for me to think that someone was actually correcting my lessons personally and paying attention to my answers. It was very special to me.

As my sister, my mom, and I became convicted about what we were learning, we started looking for a Seventh-day Adventist church. There was no Adventist church near our house, so we began to worship at home on Sabbath. We told our neighbor about the seventh-day Sabbath and our Bible lessons. She also began studying the Voice of Prophecy lessons! Eventually an Adventist pastor made the long journey to visit us. He answered our many questions. We continued our Voice of Prophecy lessons, and one beautiful Sabbath afternoon, my sister, my mom, our neighbor, and I were all baptized in the river!

Not long after that, we moved yet again. Once again, there was no Adventist church nearby, so we worshiped at home. Before long, turmoil raised its ugly head in our home once more. One night my mom woke up my sister and me, saying, "We're going away."

"Where are we going?" I asked as I climbed into the car, sleepy-eyed and in my pajamas. Our destination turned out to be a small room in a town called East Millinocket. I had to start going to a new school. I didn't want to; I liked my old school. But I didn't have a choice. A few months later, we moved again. And I had to go to still another school. This last move, however, became a real turning point in my life. We lived right next door to a Pentecostal pastor and his family. There were eight children in the family—four girls and four boys—and my sister and I began playing with these kids and doing things together. By this time, with the trauma we were going through, we were no longer worshiping on Sabbath. One day our new neighbors invited us to go to church with them on Sunday.

Well, I thought, *at least I'll get to go to church.* So, I went to church with the Pentecostal family on Sunday. I became a cheerleader at my school and attended sports events on Saturday. But somehow God was continually reminding me, *You know this isn't quite right.* Still, I was only ten years old, going on eleven. What could I do about it? There was virtually no religious instruction in my home, and, given the circumstances, I had no opportunities to worship on Sabbath.

My religious life came to a crossroad one night at a young people's meeting at the Pentecostal church. By this time, I was thirteen years old and had been attending that church for three years. At this meeting the Pentecostal pastor asked whether any of the young people would like to give their hearts to the Lord. Well, I knew that was what I wanted to do, so I stood. And when I stood, other young people also stood. Then the pastor said, "We are going to have a baptism, and I would like each of you to participate." The baptismal date was set.

The Saturday night before the scheduled Sunday baptism I went to bed just like any other night. But that night I had a dream. Now I know that God doesn't always work this way, but I believe He knew what I needed at this very moment. I believe God sent me that dream. In it, I saw the world on fire, and I saw Jesus coming in the clouds of heaven. I saw angels. Then a very clear voice spoke, which I can hear in my mind to this day. The voice said, "You are in the wrong church. You need to find a Sabbath-keeping church."

When I woke up, I told my sister about the dream. "We need to go to church," I said, "and tell the kids in our Sunday School class and our teacher about the Sabbath." So that Sunday, as a thirteen-year-old, I told them about my dream and about the seventh-day Sabbath. Their response was, "Oh Teenie, you know, it's not necessary to keep Saturday as the Sabbath. We're not under the law; we're under grace."

I remembered my Voice of Prophecy lessons. The Holy Spirit brought Isaiah 8:20 to my mind—"To the law and to the testimony: if they speak not according to this word, it is because there is no light in them." God put the words into my mouth to respond. "Yes, we are certainly saved by grace, but grace leads us to obey God's commands—not disobey them. There are ten commandments, not nine."

This created a lot of discussion! But finally everyone tried to convince me by saying, "Teenie, you need to join your friends and be baptized today."

But my response was, "No, I need to find a Sabbath-keeping church."

All the other young people were baptized that afternoon. I was the only one who was not. It was very difficult because there was so much peer pressure. They said, "Teenie, don't you love the Lord? Why aren't you going to be baptized here in our church? Don't you love the Lord?"

I said, "Yes, I *do* love the Lord, but I need to find a Sabbath-keeping church."

When I went home that day, the question in my mind was, *What do I do now?* Before I climbed into bed that night, I knelt down and prayed, "Lord, I don't know what to do. It seems like my friends are all wondering why I was not baptized. They think I'm fanatical because I wasn't baptized with everybody else." I knew the Lord wanted me to keep the Sabbath, because I had studied it in the Bible and the Bible lessons. I prayed, "Lord, You've impressed me that the Sabbath and truths I learned from the Voice of Prophecy lessons are right. Lord, somehow help me to find a Sabbath-keeping church."

Not long after this experience, my mother announced yet another move. This time we were moving to Portland, Maine. When we arrived, I thought, *I wonder if there is an Adventist church here. I wonder if there is a Sabbath-keeping church in this town.* I looked in the phone book, and to my delight, I found an entry: *Seventh-day Adventist.* I copied down the address. Later, I discovered it was the address of the Seventh-day Adventist conference office. One morning I began walking to the location I had discovered in the phone book. I had no other way to get there except to walk. I was about fourteen years old at this time. I was an outgoing teenager, but I was nervous as I walked into the building. "Hello," I greeted the receptionist. "My name is Ernestine Tenney, and I was wondering if there is a Sabbath-keeping church in this town?"

The receptionist smiled and said, "Oh, yes. There's one called the White Memorial Church over on Grant Street."

"Can you tell me how to get to Grant Street, please?" I asked. After further questioning, I discovered the church was three or four miles from where I lived.

The next Sabbath morning I dressed for church and began walking. I hadn't gone far when a car stopped beside me. The lady driving the car said, "Would you like a ride?" I quickly glanced at her and shook my head! Looking straight ahead, I continued walking.

Then the car pulled up beside me again. Again the lady asked if I would like a ride. "No thank you," I answered. Now I was afraid, so I began walking faster.

A third time, the car stopped beside me. This time, the lady said, "Are you walking to the Seventh-day Adventist church on Grant Street?"

I was shocked. I said, "Well, yes, uh . . . how do *you* know that?"

"I was at the conference office," she replied, "and I overheard you talking to the receptionist, and I recognized you walking down the road."

At that point I trusted her and climbed into the car. After that, this lady picked me up and brought me to church every Sabbath. I'll never forget that first morning when I walked into the Adventist church on Grant Street. The greeters said, "Good morning! Are you here by yourself?"

"Yes."

"Well, would you like to meet some other young people?"

"Yes."

One of the greeters introduced me to another girl about my age who showed me around the church. She took me downstairs to a room with desks in it. "What's this room?" I asked.

"It's a school," she responded.

"What kind of school?"

And she said, "This is a *church* school."

"What is a church school?"

"Well, you know, it's just a regular school run by the church."

I found out the school went through the tenth grade. I was just starting the ninth grade. I talked to one of the teachers that day at church. As the teacher explained the details about the school, I really became excited. My mind raced. I would love to go to a school like this with other Seventh-day Adventist Christian young people—a school where the Bible was taught. Then the teacher explained that each student paid tuition. My heart sank.

"I don't have any money," I said, "but I'm a hard worker, and I know how to babysit. I can earn some money. How can I make arrangements to go to this school?"

The principal of the school and school board eventually voted that I could receive tuition subsidy from the worthy-student fund. I worked hard and paid what I could. Church sponsors made up the difference. I will be forever indebted to the Adventist church and school for giving me this opportunity—and, of course, to the Voice of Prophecy for starting this entire chain of events.

I attended Portland Junior Academy in the ninth and tenth grades. That's when I started to get involved in the church. I helped with Voice of Youth evangelistic meetings and many other types of youth meetings. The church really nurtured me. Its leaders involved me. After I finished the tenth grade, I asked, "What do I do now?"

The principal of the school arranged for me to visit South Lancaster, Massachusetts—and the Adventist academy there. This was a wonderful experience for me. I had never been out of the state of Maine in my life! The teachers explained to me, "This is where you go when you're in the eleventh and twelfth grades."

I was so impressed with South Lancaster Academy and the possibility of going there. Once again, I faced the issue of money—or to state it more accurately, my lack of money!

I got a job in the book bindery. I worked seventy hours a week during the summer and thirty hours during the school year. I worked all vacations. I graduated from South Lancaster Academy and then went to Atlantic Union College. In college, I met Mark Finley, who would become my husband. When we were both sophomores in college, Mark and I had an opportunity to speak at some evangelistic meetings. As a result, the Southern New England Conference asked Mark if he would work as a pastor when he graduated. God was truly leading in our lives—leading us into evangelism.

I never dreamed when I was a little girl in Millinocket, Maine, that one day God would lead my life so miraculously. I never dreamed I would travel with my evangelist husband to almost every continent and nearly eighty countries and participate in meetings with hundreds and thousands giving their lives to Christ. That never even entered my mind. But one thing that I *did* know and determined even as a young child was that I did *not* want to live the kind of life that was thrust upon me in my childhood. I wanted God to lead my life. A person can choose the direction of his or her life. You can change things by the choices you make and by asking God to lead you. And it was God who led me all along the way. I have no question about it.

And I am so thankful for the Voice of Prophecy. It has always held a special place in my heart. If I had not taken those Voice of Prophecy Bible lessons, I don't know that I would ever have come to know or understand the Adventist message. And, you know, I understood the truth of the Bible at a very young age. It is quite amazing how the Holy Spirit leads even young people to a knowledge of His Word. He places within their hearts a deep love for Jesus. Even ten-year-olds, eleven-year-olds, and twelve-year-olds can have the spiritual conviction to make right decisions. God impressed me what to do; He impressed me to want to follow what I was learning in the lessons. Thank God for the Voice of Prophecy!

જ

Teenie Finley and her husband, Mark, have served as a team in pastoral and evangelistic ministry, including It Is Written *television. Teenie has coordinated their evangelism pre-work programs, written cookbooks and training handbooks, and preached her own evangelistic meetings. The Finleys have three children.*

Just a Dirty Scrap of Paper

Amy Smith Mapp

I'll always remember the spring of my junior year in high school. It was 1966, and I was sitting in church. We attended a first-day church, and I had become discouraged by some things I saw happening in the leadership. Certain things just didn't seem right. Because my parents were part of the leadership, I had an open door to what really went on behind closed ones. I remembered hearing the pastor say something and thinking to myself, *He's such a hypocrite!*

Immediately, I prayed a silent prayer. For the first time in my life, I prayed, *Dear Jesus, I don't think this is the church You want me to attend. If that is true, please lead me to the church You do want me to attend—and help me to know that it's Your will for me.* I prayed that prayer, but I soon focused on other things and forgot about it.

A few weeks later, I was walking with a friend down a busy street. The street was littered with crumpled, dirty scraps of paper and other

29

debris from a recent rain. One piece of paper, a little way ahead, caught my attention. Something seemed to be telling me to pick it up. The desire became stronger as I walked closer. There was paper everywhere, but this particular piece seemed to jump out at me. I picked it up. It was faded and had tire marks all over it. I could barely read the print.

It was an enrollment card for some Bible lessons by mail from some place called the Voice of Prophecy. I was a carefree teen who didn't have time to mail off something about the Bible. I threw the card on the table when I got home and left it there. A few days later, a nagging feeling led me back to it again. I sat down, filled out the card, and mailed it. The first lesson arrived on a day when I was struggling with some things in my life. The very first words of the accompanying letter spoke peace to my young heart: "Friend, are you struggling with things in your life?" I felt an instant connection.

During the next year, as the lessons arrived, I would open the package after completing my homework, and late into the night I would pour over the Scriptures, filling in the answer to each question in the lesson. The Holy Spirit became my teacher. I could feel the promptings of the Holy Spirit, helping me to understand the difficult prophecies in the books of Daniel and Revelation. I had never seen anything like this before. I accepted every truth as I studied it, including the seventh-day Sabbath. I never had a question about accepting the truth, because the printed Word came with so much conviction and power.

I completed every Bible course the Voice of Prophecy had to offer. I didn't realize at the time how hungry I was for God's Word. I treasured the personal notes of encouragement that the instructors sent with the lessons. And I didn't have to pay for anything! I thanked God for these lessons and for whoever had made it possible for me to receive them and find salvation.

Subsequently, an Adventist family invited me to some tent meetings being held in our town. I attended every night and was baptized into the Seventh-day Adventist Church. The first time I walked through the doors of the Adventist church, I heard a gentle voice whisper in my heart, "You're home now; this is where I want you to be."

Today, I am still an Adventist. I realize that long ago a simple prayer in church one Sunday was heard by a God who cares for those who are searching for Him. I still marvel at how He caused that Voice of Prophecy enrollment card to jump out at me from the street. How did it get there? Where did it come from? One day, in heaven, I will be able to meet and thank the people who sponsored my lessons, the people who corrected them, and the people who wrote such encouraging notes to me—the people who are directly responsible for helping me to know the truth as it is in Christ Jesus. And I particularly want to meet the One responsible for hearing my prayer and placing that piece of paper in the street.

There are so many people today searching for God and the truth. The Voice of Prophecy stands as a beacon in a dark night, guiding people home. Praise God for this ministry!

℃℈

Amy Smith Mapp lives in Montgomery, Alabama, where she serves as the prayer ministries director and chaplain of the Women's Ministries Executive Committee of the Gulf States Conference. Amy is a retired educator and adjunct university professor. She and her husband, Bernell, have three children.

Saved From the Fire!

Derek J. Morris

Some sixty years ago, my parents, Colin and Fleur Morris, were visiting my grandmother. My parents were just a young couple at the time. As my mother and grandmother were talking, my father picked up a black-and-white card lying near the fireplace. The card offered Bible study lessons from the Voice of Prophecy. As he was examining the card, my grandmother came into the room looking for it. She intended to use it to light the fire! My father asked her if, instead, he could mail it in and request the lessons. "Yes," grandmother said. "It was under the front door when I came home. I started to throw it away, but then I kept it to light the fire."

So began a long spiritual journey that started before I was born. My parents began studying with the Voice of Prophecy by mail and completed two series of lessons. The local pastor, Peter Stearman, came to visit and gave my parents further Bible studies in their home. Shortly after I was born, my parents, previously active in the Baptist church, were rebaptized into the Seventh-day Adventist Church in Bristol, England.

They never discovered who slid the card through grandmother's door—probably some dear soul waiting for the bus at the stop a few houses away. As a result of that one Voice of Prophecy enrollment card, my parents went to Newbold College, and my father became a pastor-evangelist. He worked for fifteen years in England before receiving a call to be an Adventist pastor in America. My older brother emigrated to Australia and then on to New Zealand. I also went to Newbold College, where I met my future bride, Bodil Chen. Bodil and I were married in Takoma Park, Maryland, and continued our studies at Andrews University.

My ministry has included pastoring churches in Pennsylvania, California, and Florida, teaching at Southern Adventist University in Tennessee, and serving as associate ministerial secretary of the General Conference in Silver Spring, Maryland, and editor of *Ministry*, an international journal for pastors. In person and through the media ministry of Hope Sabbath School and *Ministry in Motion*, I have been able to train thousands of pastors and lay members in more than 130 countries around the world.

That single little Voice of Prophecy enrollment card has resulted in two pastor-evangelists and hundreds of individuals baptized into the Seventh-day Adventist Church around the world—and the results are still continuing! How amazed that dear soul will be on the resurrection morning to learn about the results of the little card he or she slipped under my grandmother's door in England so long ago! More than a card was saved from the fire!

✑

Derek J. Morris serves as an associate ministerial secretary of the General Conference, and editor of Ministry *magazine, an international journal for pastors. He is seen frequently on Hope Channel teaching Hope Sabbath School and co-hosts* MINISTRYinMOTION. *Derek and his wife, Bodil, have two children.*

The Voice of Prophecy Saved My Marriage and Changed My Life

Roma Paley Ohman

In 1975 my marriage was at the breaking point. I didn't know what to do. Should Dave and I stay together and try to make another go of our marriage? Would it be better if we separated and went our own ways? Eventually, Dave went to his parents' home while we tried to sort things out. With their father gone, our two children sensed that all was not well; they became disobedient and unsettled. I was in turmoil during this time, trying to decide what would be best in the long term.

Dave returned home a few days later saying he wanted us to try again to make the marriage work. I agreed verbally, but in my heart I was not convinced that things would improve.

The following weekend, my sister and brother-in-law came to visit. They tried to help, but after talking with us late into the night, they decided that our relationship had broken down too badly to be mended.

I went to bed that night unable to settle my jumbled thoughts. I felt such turmoil inside; I just wanted to have peace somehow. Dave came into the room and found me in an agitated state. He offered to have my sister come and talk with me. All I wanted was for someone to give me something to allow me to sleep so that I wouldn't have to deal with the continual inner conflict and indecision I was experiencing. In my mind, I cried out, *Oh, God!* I didn't realize at the time that it was a prayer.

Six years previously I had attended the local Congregational church for about a year and had found it difficult to understand the Bible. Dave had never been interested in discussing the Bible or religious things, and as my life changed, I stopped going to church.

My sister came into the bedroom around 2:00 A.M. and sat and talked with me. During our conversation, I gradually began to ask myself: *What has happened to our marriage relationship? I loved Dave when we got married; where has that love gone?* We had both changed since then, but I wondered if maybe there was something that could be salvaged from our relationship. As my sister and I talked, the thought came to me that God had forgiven me for the bad things I had done in my life. I hadn't asked Him to forgive me; I just *knew* He had.

At 6:00 A.M. I suddenly felt convinced that God wanted Dave and me to stay together and try to continue our marriage. I didn't know how it would work out. All I knew was that God wanted us to be together, which was all I needed to know at the time.

I experienced an overwhelming peace at that moment, and all my inner turmoil disappeared. I thought, *If this is the peace that we'll have in heaven, then it's worth waiting for.* My sister later said that it looked as though an unseen hand had taken all my troubles away and that she, too, felt real peace and calm in the room. Although she and I had been talking for four hours, it seemed like only a few minutes. She went to let Dave know that he could come to see me now—and found him and her husband asleep. When Dave awoke, he knew something was different even before my sister spoke to him. He could sense the peace in the house, and my brother-in-law noticed it, too, when he awoke.

Dave came upstairs to see me, and all I could talk about was God's peace and how wonderful it was. That God wanted us to stay together and that although I didn't know how things would work out, I knew it was the right thing to do. And God would be with us.

The next day, because my nerves were all on edge, the children and I went to stay with my sister to give me some time to recover. I returned home a week later with a desire to read the Bible. This time, it was a different experience from my earlier efforts. It was as if the Bible had come to life and had begun to make sense to me! However, I found the language of the King James Version hard to understand. I decided I needed to read the Bible in a modern English translation. I knew of only one neighbor on my street who might possess such a book. I asked her about it, and although she didn't have such a Bible, she did have a book *about* the Bible. It was titled *Your Bible and You.* She loaned this book to me; I read it and wanted a copy of my own. My neighbor told me she had bought the book from a woman who had sold it to her at the door seven years previously. Miraculously, she still had the receipt with the woman's telephone number on it!

I called the number and reached Gladys Brailsford. She said she would come to visit me. I later learned that she was a part-time literature evangelist. To my surprise, I discovered that Gladys had sold *me* some children's books at the same time she had sold *Your Bible and You* to my neighbor! At that time, seven years earlier, both my neighbor and I had lived on opposite sides of a different housing project and had not known each other. Now we had both moved to a new housing project and lived on opposite sides of the same street!

I asked Gladys if she could get me a Bible in modern English—instead of *Your Bible and You.* She said she would be happy to bring one the following week. Before she left, she asked if I would be interested studying the Bible by mail through the Voice of Prophecy. It would help me understand the Bible, she assured me.

Meanwhile, I kept reading the King James Bible and shared what I was learning with Dave. He became interested and wanted a Bible of his own. The following week, when Gladys returned with my Bible, Dave ordered one for himself.

When the first lessons arrived from the Voice of Prophecy, Dave and

I started to work through them. I found that first lesson *so hard*. I had to read and reread each question and struggle to find the answer in the Bible. It took me two weeks to complete that lesson. I thought I would receive a bad grade and felt very discouraged about the project.

Imagine my delight when the lesson came back in the mail and I discovered that I had gotten an A, with "Well done" written on the page! I eagerly started the second lesson, and although it sometimes took me a while to understand, I never found another lesson as difficult as that first one. I realize now that the enemy of God was trying to discourage me.

Every two weeks, Dave and I received our lessons, faithfully marked and returned to us along with new ones to complete. Each week Gladys came with a tape by Pastor George Vandeman, which she played for us. Often the tape would address a subject similar to the one we were studying in the current Voice of Prophecy lesson.

As Dave and I read and discussed the Bible, we drew closer to God. And as we drew closer to Him, we also drew closer to each other. The rift in our relationship was replaced with a deeper, more forgiving and understanding relationship than we had ever had in the past. Our love for each other revived and grew.

We purchased the *Bible Stories* and other books for our children. It was quite amazing to us how God worked to reunite a family that had been so badly broken, using various means to reach and teach us.

In 1976, Dave and I were baptized into the Seventh-day Adventist Church. We spent many happy years together until Dave died in 2003. However, he died knowing that one day Jesus will come and take him home to live with Him forever. He knew his Savior, and I am so thankful for that! Without the Voice of Prophecy lessons we would not have learned to search the Bible for ourselves. The lessons showed us the texts in the Bible to answer our questions and help us see a more detailed picture of God. They taught us to search the Scriptures for ourselves, comparing scripture with scripture in order to gain a better understanding. Thanks to the Voice of Prophecy lessons and Gladys's encouragement, our knowledge of the God who has the power to change broken lives increased day by day.

The Voice of Prophecy played an important role in our getting to know God. When someone on the correspondence school staff writes, "Well done!" or "Good" on a student's completed lesson, I can tell you that it is extremely encouraging. It adds a personal touch, and the student realizes that there is a real live person at the other end. I know now that the staff at the Voice of Prophecy were praying for us and that many times when we were struggling to learn the truth, their prayers on our behalf were being answered. I thank God for that and for the dedicated men and women who operate the Bible correspondence schools!

cx

Roma Ohman lives with her husband, Sven, in Kettering, Northamptonshire, England. Roma has two children by her late husband, David Paley, and five grandchildren. She has served the Trans-European Division office since 1988, as receptionist and secretary to various departments.

Oklahoma Surprise

Ken Cox

Farming in the southeast corner of Oklahoma is a hot, dusty affair in summer. Our family—my father, Otto, my mother, Laura, my sister, Dorothy, and I—lived on twenty acres on which we grew corn and potatoes. One spring afternoon, while we were away from home, a man came by handing out copies of *These Times*® magazine.*

Because no one was home at our place, he stopped at a neighbor's home a half mile down the road. After talking with the man, Mrs. Morgan took the copy of the magazine he offered. When he left, she glanced through it but didn't find anything of interest to her. So she inserted it inside a Sears Roebuck catalog.

Now, our family was Baptist. That is, we went to the Baptist church once in a while, but we were really what you would call nominal Christians.

---

* *These Times*® was published simultaneously with *Signs of the Times*® magazines. Today, *Signs* covers the original purpose of both magazines.

A few days later, my mother stopped by Mrs. Morgan's house to ask if she could borrow her Sears Roebuck catalog. Arriving home, she began thumbing through the catalog and came across the copy of *These Times*® inside. She began looking through the magazine with interest. One article, especially, caught her attention. It dealt with the topic of the Sabbath and which day of the week is the biblical day of worship.

After reading this article, Mother was so impressed—and troubled—that she immediately headed for the field where my dad and I were plowing with the horses, getting the ground ready for planting. As Mom came walking across the newly plowed ground, her dress moving with the breeze, Dad saw her coming and stopped the horses. She and Dad sat down together in the field, using the horses for shade, and read that article about the Sabbath. It was new information to them—both interesting and troubling.

When Mother returned Mrs. Morgan's catalog, she asked about the magazine that had been inside it. Hearing the story, she asked her neighbor to send the man to her house if he came by again with more magazines. Sure enough, as a faithful servant for God, Brother Morses stopped by our house some time later and introduced himself to the family. We all began Bible studies together, and eventually Mom and I signed up for the Voice of Prophecy Bible lessons.

Dad didn't accept the Sabbath. He refused to go to the Adventist church with us and began to oppose our following the Bible truths we were learning. Mother, Dorothy, and I persevered and were baptized in the McAlester, Oklahoma, Seventh-day Adventist Church. I was sixteen years old at the time. Soon the situation at home became quite difficult—so bad, in fact, that my father would whip me when I came home from church. So a year later, I decided to go away to school. Knowing Dad would never permit me to do so, I left home one morning when he was gone. With twenty-two cents in my pocket, I hitchhiked to Southwestern Junior College in Keene, Texas. When I arrived on campus, I simply told the people there that I had come to attend school and that I needed a job! God led and enabled me to get an education there that would make it possible for me to serve Him in the ministry.

It's amazing what God can do! Today, Kenneth Cox Ministries is dedicated to preaching the Word through public evangelism, television, radio, books, and leaflets—any method that we can use to reach men and women for Jesus Christ. Through the Lord's blessing, our programs are viewed on television stations across the nation.

ᐔ

Kenneth Cox has served as pastor and evangelist, conducting numerous field schools of evangelism for pastors and laypeople. He has preached evangelistic meetings worldwide, personally and via DVD and television. Ken lives in Tennessee and has four children.

Mom's Stay-at-Home Plan

Kurt Johnson

"Mom, do we have to go to church today? Can't we stay home? Dad has to take the car to work, anyway."

"If you stay home, you will have to study a Bible lesson before you can go outside and go sledding."

"OK!"

Later that day, with my two sisters and my brother, I was heading to the sledding hill across the street from our house on the outskirts of Murray, Utah. I was twelve years old, and our family had just moved to Utah from Washington State. Skipping church and the pastor's sermon was all right with me. It seemed that all the pastor was interested in was baptizing me. The kids at church had their own group of friends—and, being new, I wasn't part of the group.

In fact, with Dad sometimes working six days a week, and with just one car in the family, transportation to church was, at times, a challenge. Our family was deeply anchored in God. Family worship, singing hymns while

Mom strummed her guitar, prayer, and a deep faith was part of the family routine. This included Dad, who didn't go to church himself but wanted to make sure his kids were raised with church and God as part of their upbringing. When we asked Dad why he stayed home from church while the rest of the family attended, he'd respond, "I went to church when I was a kid, and so will you."

Mom, however, had a plan in mind if the family was unable to attend church on a given week. You see, she had studied the Voice of Prophecy Bible lessons as a teenager. My great-grandma had introduced her to the lessons. Great-grandma was a Seventh-day Adventist, and Great-grandpa was a Methodist. In fact, on my dad's side of the family, two great-uncles were Methodist ministers. So Mom's stay-at-home-from-church plan was simple: my brother and sisters and I had to enroll in a Voice of Prophecy Bible course and study one lesson on Saturday morning before heading outdoors to swing on the rope hanging from a limb of the old oak tree or play in the snow with the neighborhood kids.

But for me, studying the Bible lessons soon became more than just what I did when we were not able to attend church. I developed a growing interest in the Bible and began studying the lessons regularly. During a three-year period, I completed several Voice of Prophecy courses including *Bright Horizons, Light of the World, Faith,* and *Bible Prophecy.* The textbook for the prophecy course was Uriah Smith's *Daniel and Revelation.* As a fifteen-year-old, I read the book from cover to cover. Mom's stay-at-home-plan changed my life.

I accepted Jesus as my Lord and Savior after completing the Light of the World course. I knew for a fact that Saturday was the Sabbath once I completed the *Faith* course. But I still had unanswered questions about God and the Bible. After the prophecy lessons on Daniel 2, I was convinced that God truly existed and that the Bible was His authentic Word. Between the ages of twelve and fifteen I enjoyed spending time at the kitchen table with a Voice of Prophecy lesson much more than I did attending church. Looking back, I believe that experience was the best thing that could have happened to me. As I studied God's Word, it spoke to my mind and heart. One cannot read God's Word and not be changed.

The summer I turned fifteen, our family moved to Yuma, Arizona. I was just completing the Daniel and Revelation course. The youth leaders at the Yuma Adventist Church quickly took the Johnson kids under their wing. My brother and sisters and I felt like we belonged. It was a time when the Holy Spirit took the information I had learned from the Voice of Prophecy Bible courses, along with other influences, and brought me to a point of decision in my life. Between the influence of Mom and Dad at home, Sabbath School, prayer meeting, and other activities, it wasn't long until I decided I wanted to be baptized. So, on a sunny Yuma Sabbath morning in June, the deacons moved the pulpit, rolled back the carpet, removed the planks covering the baptismal tank—and my sister Caren and I were baptized.

The wooden steps down into the baptistry were old and beginning to deteriorate. My sister and I made it down into the baptistry safely and were baptized by Pastor Gordon McCrillis. We were not so lucky on the way out. As my sister stepped onto the middle step, the years took their toll on the rotting wood and the step broke! With the help of the deacons and with banana-size smiles on our faces, we safely made it out of the water. But it still brings laughter when we talk about it today.

A couple of weeks later, our family moved back to the Northwest. I enrolled at Pasco High School for the beginning of my junior year. Soon I became convicted that God wanted me to be a minister. It was quite a struggle, because I was very shy. Mrs. Davidson, a committed Christian woman who taught my high-school speech class, encouraged me to follow my conviction. She had several personal talks with me, telling me to pray about it and to trust God's leading. She told me she believed I had the speaking ability to become a preacher. Her encouragement had a marked influence upon me.

Today, as I look back on my decision for Christ and eventually my decision to become a minister, I know that God used the Voice of Prophecy Bible School as a significant influence in that process. In an interesting sequence of events, H. M. S. Richards Sr. the founder of the Voice of Prophecy, preached at my ordination service and was part of the ordination prayer and laying on of hands. Little did we both know that nineteen years later I would become the International Bible

School director for the Voice of Prophecy! Today, it's my privilege to direct the work of the Bible School—the very agency that God used as part of my journey to lead me to Him and to His truth!

 co

Kurt Johnson has served as a pastor and in departmental positions throughout his ministry. He currently serves as Voice of Prophecy Bible School director for the North American Division and coordinates Bible correspondence schools for the General Conference. Kurt and his wife, Janey, have two children.

Once Upon a Cold, Wintry Storm

Larry Boggess

A typical Ohio 1950s winter storm had dumped inches and inches of snow on the ground all over the state, but particularly on the eastern part, bringing everything to a halt. Roads were shut down, and all one could do was to stay inside where it was warm. Due to the storm, Everett and Mildred Boggess and their family of six children were unable to attend Sunday services at their nearby Methodist church. The Boggess family lived on a farm, and that morning the children were told that as soon as the farm animals were cared for and fed, the family would have Sunday School and church—at home!

Once chores were finished and the animals' needs were met, Everett and Mildred conducted Sunday School for the five sons, three of whom were teenagers, and their young daughter. After "Sunday School," Mildred played hymns on the piano while the family sang. Then everyone gathered around the radio. Everett began turning the dial to find a preacher so the family could hear a sermon for the morning church service. He stopped the dial when he heard a quartet singing religious music. The family had never heard of the King's Heralds, so they had no idea that was the name of the quartet they were listening to. After the music, a preacher began speaking. Everett and Mildred were impressed with his message and with this broadcast called the *Voice of Prophecy*. At the end of the sermon, the preacher—H. M. S. Richards Sr.—offered free Bible lessons to study at home. This offer particularly interested Everett, because he had recently accepted Jesus as his Savior.

Everett wrote to the address given on the broadcast, asking to enroll in the Bible course. The lessons began arriving in the mailbox, and the family studied them together, filling out the answer sheets and returning them. It wasn't long until they had finished all the lessons. At this point, Brother Farber, a Bible worker from the Canton, Ohio, Seventh-day Adventist Church, came to the Boggesses' farm and began studying the Bible with the family. About a year after tuning in to the *Voice of Prophecy* broadcast that wintry, stormy Sunday, the Boggess family was baptized into the Seventh-day Adventist Church.

This was in the early 1950s. Everett and Mildred later became charter members of the Carrollton, Ohio, Seventh-day Adventist Church, which they raised up with the help of another couple in an adjoining county. Everett passed away at the age of ninety-six on Christmas morning 2008—a farmer turned businessman, literature evangelist, and church planter. He was preceded in death by Mildred, his faithful, lifetime friend and wife who died in 1994. Everett and Mildred were the parents of three Seventh-day Adventist ministers, Robert, Larry, and Ben, and a church school teacher, Janet, as well as three other children, Danny, Richard, and Jo'An. They were grandparents of one Adventist minister, Tom, two church-school teachers, Bruce and Mari Ann Boggess Burns, and two other denominationally employed workers, John David and Darla. All this resulted from the Holy Spirit using a winter storm and the *Voice of Prophecy* radio broadcast to guide the Boggess family to the Adventist message!

Who could have known what the Lord had in store for the Boggess family that cold wintry morning? Only in heaven will be revealed the hundreds, perhaps thousands, who have come to know Jesus through the ministry of this family who first heard the Adventist message through the Voice of Prophecy broadcast and Bible school!

&

Larry Boggess has served as pastor, evangelist, publishing director, Adventist Book Center manager, and church administrator. He is currently the president of the Mountain View Conference, which includes West Virginia and a portion of Maryland. Larry and his wife, Joan, have three children.

A Pearl of Great Price

Joyce Johnson

Although the postman had delivered the mail in her neighborly community for more than twenty years with complete accuracy, his delivery error one fall day in 1958 would change Gladys Johnson's life—and the lives of her family—forever. That day, Gladys was surprised to discover an item in her mailbox that was addressed to a nearby neighbor. She was about to return the small pamphlet to the mailbox for re-routing when she noticed the words:

Where are you going to spend eternity?

She was deeply intrigued. The question inspired her to read on, hoping to find an answer that would satisfy her deep longing for a closer walk with God. Gladys had been reared in a Christian home where she had been taught about God's amazing love, yet she yearned for complete assurance that her life was fully aligned with His Word. She had been earnestly praying for a deeper relationship with God; she even had a special place for prayer—a remote site on the family farm in Collierville, Tennessee. Little did she know that the answer to her prayer for a renewed life in Christ would come in a small piece of missorted mail.

Prayerfully and carefully, Gladys read every word of the Voice of Prophecy Bible guide that had appeared in her mailbox. Its captivating message, filled with Bible texts and thought-provoking questions, created a desire in her heart for more of the same. After reading the study guide, she copied the address of the Voice of Prophecy and returned the treasured piece of mail to her mailbox to be delivered to its rightful recipient. Then she wrote, asking to receive the Bible study guides herself.

Soon the first study guide appeared in her mailbox—addressed, this time, to her! Gladys carefully studied lesson after lesson, comparing them with the Bible. As she learned truths from God's Word, she made decisions to follow what she was learning and put these things into practice in her life—including changes in her diet and following what seemed to her to be an unusual day of worship. The Voice of Prophecy even arranged a visit from the pastor of a nearby church that followed the biblical teachings that Gladys was learning and embracing—the Mississippi Boulevard Seventh-day Adventist Church in Memphis, Tennessee.

The very next week, Gladys visited the church for the very first time in response to Pastor Charles Graham's invitation. The day of worship was like no other that she had ever experienced. Although it happened many years ago, Gladys always remembered the delectable Sabbath luncheon, the warm hugs and greetings, and the soul-stirring sermon about God's saving grace. Responding to the pastor's appeal, Gladys took her stand for Jesus and His truth. A baptism was scheduled for the very next week. She had finally found what she'd been seeking her entire life, and the effects would be far-reaching.

The spark from that misdirected mail has since flamed into more than thirty baptisms of family members and friends. Until her death at the age of ninety-five in October 2012, Gladys faithfully and untiringly proclaimed God's love and His soon return! She knew beyond any doubt that the Bible study guide from the Voice of Prophecy that showed up in her mailbox so many years ago was not at all misdirected. Rather, it was God-directed! To her, it was the pearl of great price that Jesus mentions in Matthew 13:46. It was also a miraculous fulfillment of God's promise in Jeremiah 29:13: "And ye shall seek me, and find me, when ye shall search for me with all your heart."

Praise God for the faithful and timely ministry of the Voice of Prophecy! Through God's Holy Spirit and Gladys Johnson's earnest seeking, the Voice of Prophecy enabled her to find the pearl of great price.

❧

Joyce Johnson, PhD, is Gladys Johnson's daughter. She currently serves as a university professor. Her husband, Washington, DMin, is a chaplain in the United States Navy and a Seventh-day Adventist minister. The Johnsons have a son, Washington III.

The Gift Goes On

E. Lonnie Melashenko

No doubt about it! God's holy Word saved me. Protected me. Shielded me. Transformed me. Revived me. Who knows where I might have wandered in life had it not been for the Bible and the Voice of Prophecy Bible School. The smorgasbord of correspondence lessons I took during my critical impressionable growing-up years helped me deal with so many issues and temptations.

My parents moved from Saskatchewan to Springfield, Massachusetts, in 1957 when I was just ten years old. Some of my young friends were experimenting with questionable activities. I grew up on a farm in Canada, far removed from such fascinating, but inappropriate, vices that my new American city friends considered fun—this was challenging for me! Attractive. Tempting.

Providentially, a few of my young friends at church school were talking about baptism. When I expressed interest, my parents and

the local pastor, Wylie Fowler, encouraged me to enroll in the Voice
of Prophecy's Junior Bible lessons. In those years there were no pre-
baptismal lessons for kids, so most junior-age children took the
Voice of Prophecy lessons to prepare for baptism. I had to earn
money with a paper route to afford the postage for mailing the lessons back and forth, but I treasured my certificate when it arrived.
The following year, pastor-evangelist Garnet Williams was conducting a series of evangelistic meetings at our church. I attended
faithfully and subsequently made my decision to be baptized at the
tender age of eleven, a decision I have never regretted. My parents
were thrilled.

During my young teenage years in the islands of Bermuda, I attended a public high school since there was no Christian academy
available. My parents were concerned for their eldest son—specifically
about the movies and the dances that all my classmates participated
in and the influences surrounding me. What to do? They felt their
prayers were answered when I found great delight in signing up for
several Voice of Prophecy Bible correspondence courses. I eagerly
studied them instead of becoming interested in the theater and other
distractions. Long before e-mail and iPads or cell phones, mail was a
big deal for a teenager! Most lessons were not sent by air mail, which
was too costly in those days, so it took awhile to receive and send
lessons back and forth to America. But during our family's three years
of mission service in the "Isles of Rest," I anticipated receiving new
lessons in the mail from the *Bright Horizon* course, the *Twentieth
Century* course, the courses on the Spirit of Prophecy and Daniel and
the Revelation. I studied hard in order to receive personal handwrit-
ten notes of commendation across the top of my lessons from each
of my instructors all the way across the ocean and North America in
far-off Glendale, California, where the Voice of Prophecy broadcast
headquarters was located. I carefully saved and treasured each new
certificate. I still have them.

Before studying the various Voice of Prophecy Bible courses, I had
read the Bible only casually. After I began studying, I read it all the
way through once to get credit for a required assignment. The topics

covered in each of the Voice of Prophecy courses deeply impressed me that there really are biblical answers to today's questions. I remember how touched I was at the Scripture passages that so clearly delineated the seventh-day Sabbath—when it begins, how it should be kept, how God's people will enjoy the Sabbath throughout eternity. My non-Adventist high-school friends—and even some teachers too—would ask me questions about my faith. They were impressed that a teenager had a basic working knowledge about the Bible and religious matters. God's timing is so amazing! He knew I needed to be enrolled in those Voice of Prophecy lessons during that specific phase of my life. No doubt, studying the Scriptures was also shaping my future career. Because of my growing appreciation for spiritual values, I began thinking about becoming a pastor, even during my teenage years.

I grew up in the home of a singing evangelist. My parents taught their five sons to sing in four-part harmony when we were only children. Despite our shyness, we soon found ourselves catapulted in front of church congregations, country clubs, prisons, nursing homes, and subsequently even performing live onstage for television on several occasions. Before we were teenagers, we sang before twenty thousand people at the Atlantic City Youth Congress in 1960. I still treasure my autograph book from those days. At the Youth Congress I was able to get H. M. S. Richards' autograph, together with that of Del Delker, Brad and Olive Braley, and other Voice of Prophecy celebrities. The fact that I already "knew" some of these individuals from my Voice of Prophecy Bible correspondence lessons made it even more thrilling.

Knowing that my dad had sung bass in the King's Heralds Quartet from 1948 to 1950 made me feel proud to "reconnect" with the Voice of Prophecy. In later years, Dad would become an evangelist for the Voice of Prophecy Evangelistic Association. His pastoral influence upon my decision to become a minister and attend La Sierra College played a huge part in my life. In my wildest imagination I could never have dreamed that one day—forty years later—I would walk into the same Voice of Prophecy broadcast studios and speak behind the same microphone in the recording studios as director-speaker for the Voice of Prophecy. But I did from 1991 through 2008.

During my first years as a pastoral intern, my senior pastor, Dr. John Robertson, assigned me to conduct my very own series of evangelistic meetings in Glendale, California. I went into seclusion to come up with my own series of twenty-six sermons, looking for topics that would be relevant to the current times. How does a twenty-one-year-old preach on relevant topics during the hippie era? Drugs and LSD and "love-ins" and the rock culture wildly confused millions of young Americans as the Vietnam War heated up. Young people were involved in the hippie culture of Hollywood and Haight-Ashbury in San Francisco. Old-fashioned preaching? Would it work? I fell on my knees to ask God for help. I will confess here for the first time where I went for source material for those sermons! I carefully sifted through the Voice of Prophecy's *Wayout* magazine—lessons specifically designed to address the major issues the drug culture was confronting during those troublesome '60s and '70s. Then to top it off, what a thrill it was to invite the King's Heralds Quartet, Del Delker, Walter Arties, and the Heritage Singers to perform during my meetings and witness nearly thirty-five individuals, many of them youth or young adults, make their decisions to be baptized as a result of that series! One of them, Kathy Hollister, still works for the Voice of Prophecy today.

God's holy Word is life-transforming. Seeds planted in the fertile ground of my young heart sprouted and grew to maturity, profoundly influencing my decisions and commitment to serve Jesus as a world ambassador for the great Husbandman. Jeannie and I consider ourselves greatly enriched during our eighteen years of ministry at the Voice of Prophecy as we were able to travel worldwide and witness firsthand the influence of the Voice of Prophecy and its Bible School. The Voice of Prophecy Bible School is still changing the lives of millions—one day at a time, one life at a time, one lesson at a time.

And the gift goes on . . .

ℰↄ

*Lonnie Melashenko and his wife, Jeannie, have served as pastor, asso-
ciate speaker with It Is Written, speaker-director of the Voice of Prophecy,
and vice president for Spiritual Services
and Missions, Kettering Health Network.
Currently he serves as a revivalist for the
Columbia Union.*

The Very First VOP Bible School Graduate

Kurt Johnson

Imagine that it is Sunday night, February 1, 1942. America has just become involved in World War II as a result of Japan's bombing of Pearl Harbor some two months earlier. But tonight, six men stand in place at their radio microphones waiting to broadcast live across North America.

In 1942, radio was *king*! Every home had a radio, but television sets and a telephone in every home were still in the future. On this particular Sunday night, the announcer of the radio broadcast, Fordyce Detamore, introduced the Bible correspondence school concept. In those days it was called "The Bible School of the Air." The plan was simple. Send in an enrollment card or letter and begin receiving free Bible lessons by mail. On that Sunday evening in 1942, Max (Mack) Zolnerzak, the man who was destined to become the very first graduate of the Voice of Prophecy Bible School of the Air, was still some two months away from being drafted into the United States Army.

Mack was born on November 15, 1914; one of a family of four boys. He grew up in Pittsburgh, Pennsylvania. Like thousands of young American men, Mack received his draft notice in those early days of World War II; in April 1942, he found himself in the army. While stationed at Akron, Ohio, Mack met an Adventist literature evangelist at the YMCA. Before Mack was sent to England in October 1942, the literature evangelist visited him several times. The Voice of Prophecy Bible School of the Air was only a few months old when the literature evangelist enrolled Mack in the first Voice of Prophecy (VOP) Bible lessons.

The Bible School of the Air was a success from the beginning. It was the first time anything like this had ever been tried, and the idea of studying the Bible by mail spread like wildfire. By the end of the first month, two thousand people had enrolled. By June 1942, the Bible course had been prepared in Braille. Within a few months, seventy-five thousand people were studying the Bible lessons. Within a year, the Bible School went international with correspondence schools in Central America, South America, and South Africa. The first languages that the VOP lessons were translated into were Spanish, Portuguese, German, French, Italian, Russian, and Chinese.

Meanwhile, Mack Zolnerzak, stationed in England, completed the Bible course and became the very first VOP Bible School graduate! Following his military service in England, France, and Germany, Mack returned to the United States. He had earned a college degree in elementary education before going into the army, so following his discharge from the army, Mack began teaching at elementary and junior high schools in California. It was the beginning of a career that would span more than thirty years. He later earned a master's degree in education from California State University in Turlock, California.

Even though he regularly attended the Seventh-day Adventist Church, Mack described himself as "elusive." "I never smoked or did anything bad," he recalled, but it wasn't until February 24, 1973—some thirty years after taking the VOP Bible lessons—that Mack was baptized by Alfredo Matar during an evangelistic series conducted by Duane Corwin and Jerry Dill in Merced, California.

Sadly, Mack's teaching career came to an end when diabetes left him blind. Through the years he enjoyed writing letters of encouragement to people connected with church work and to hundreds of college students. With these letters he often enclosed a dollar bill or two. He distributed hundreds of Bible course enrollment cards and other gospel literature. He especially enjoyed writing to the VOP and receiving letters and the *VOP News* in return. Because he was blind, visitors read the letters and magazines to him.

Mack Zolnerzak passed away November 20, 2004, in Atwater, California. He was the first in a very long line of men and women, and boys and girls, who have found peace of mind and faith in God through the VOP Bible School.

Here are several letters that came to the Bible School in those first few months back in 1942:

A woman in Philadelphia was planning to commit suicide. She listened to the broadcast and signed up for the Bible course. Her life was saved, and she wrote: "These Bible lessons are priceless. I can hardly wait to get the next lesson. May God help you to bring to many others the same hope you have brought to me."

A man from Los Angeles wrote, "Truly, I never knew how to study the Bible until I began taking this wonderful correspondence course. I am glad to tell you that I am being baptized in a few days."

From San Antonio, Texas, a woman wrote: "For three years I have prayed for my husband, and my prayers are being answered. Recently, he was in a railway station and found one of the lessons on prophecy. He read it through, and now he wants to enroll in your Bible course. Please keep on praying."

And the stories are still coming in today! Currently, there are Bible schools and affiliates in nearly 140 countries and lessons in more than a hundred languages and dialects. The total number of students over the years is in the countless millions! Graduates are multimillions. The number of decisions for Jesus and baptism are known only to God, but this we know—scores of people will be in the kingdom of heaven because of the work of the VOP Bible School.

Ed Zirkwitz

The Five-Hundred-Thousandth Graduate

Kurt Johnson

Edwin E. Zirkwitz, 21, left, Vancouver, British Columbia, receives the half-million-diploma issued by The Voice of Prophecy's English Bible school. W. W.

By 1960, eighteen years after the Voice of Prophecy Bible School of the Air (now called the Voice of Prophecy Discover Bible School) began offering Bible lessons by mail in 1942, the number of graduates of the English language Bible course had reached one hundred thousand. Only eleven years later, Edwin E. Zirkwitz, then a twenty-one-year-old student at Simon Fraser University in Vancouver, British Columbia, finished the Faith Bible course in August 1971 to become the five-hundred-thousandth person to graduate from the English language Bible school—marking a milestone of a half-million graduates!

Ed happened upon the *Voice of Prophecy* broadcast on radio station KARI operating out of Bellingham, Washington, and easily heard in Vancouver, B.C. "I loved H. M. S. Richards' golden voice," he recalls, "especially compared to many of the religious speakers who seemed to shriek. Also, I found the Voice of Prophecy theme song—'Lift Up the Trumpet'—appealing."

When Ed heard the broadcast offer a free Bible course by mail, he decided to enroll. "I took the Faith Bible course," he says, "and when I finished that, I enrolled in another course, but I've forgotten the name of those lessons. I was happy with what I was learning about the Bible. And I was encouraged because I was getting the answers right!  This helped me realize that the Bible wasn't as hard to understand as I had believed." Ed wasn't attending any church when he began taking the VOP Bible courses. But after completing the lessons, he was baptized into the Seventh-day Adventist Church on November 6, 1971, in Vancouver, B.C. He has remained an active Adventist ever since.

Ed was born in Edmonton, Alberta, and after living in several Canadian provinces, put down roots in Royston, B.C., on Vancouver Island when he retired from his career as an accountant and corporate manager in 2005. He and his wife, Cynthia, have been married forty-two years and have two sons and two granddaughters, Alyza and Angelika. He enjoys travel and is an avid reader. Ed currently does some part-time accounting and consulting work and enjoys going on Maranatha Volunteer International Mission Trips.

Ed will never forget becoming the five-hundred-thousandth graduate of the VOP English language Bible school—or the change the VOP has made in his life!

Victoria Fullbright

One-Millionth Bible School Graduate

Kurt Johnson

Victoria Fullbright of Hickory, North Carolina, is the one-millionth person in North America to graduate from the Voice of Prophecy Bible Correspondence School! Victoria and the Voice of Prophecy Bible School reached this milestone in mid-2010.

As a child, Victoria attended Sunday School, where the Bible stories she heard helped her grow in her relationship with God. Later, in her teen years, she attended church only sporadically for a time, but she always believed in God.

In the early part of 2009 Victoria was going through a very difficult time. One day, in the midst of these problems, she found in her mailbox the first Discover Bible guide from the Voice of Prophecy—"We Can Believe in God." She had not requested these Discover guides and had no idea who sent them to her. "They just appeared," Victoria says.

Victoria was intrigued by the Bible guide she found in her mailbox. Even though she was living a busy life as a twenty-year-old college student working on a B.S. degree in nursing, she studied the lesson, filled out the answer sheet, and mailed it back to the Voice of Prophecy. Soon she was engaged in studying the Bible with interest. Her instructor at the Bible correspondence school, Anna, sent Victoria notes of encouragement and provided prayerful support. Her interest and concern were a significant part of Victoria's Bible study experience.

One Sabbath morning in September 2009, Victoria woke up early under deep conviction that today was the day she should attend church. Sleepy-eyed, she sat down at her computer and searched for the address of the local Seventh-day Adventist church in her hometown of Hickory, North Carolina. She drove to the church and entered apprehensively. But the church members greeted her warmly. As she sat down in the back pew, a lady immediately sat down beside her, making Victoria feel welcomed and wanted.

After church, Victoria met Pastor Marc Swearingen. Pastor Marc made an appointment to visit in her home and was soon studying with, and encouraging, Victoria in her continuing search for Bible truth. Meanwhile, the friendliness and love of the Hickory church family anchored Victoria in her newly discovered faith. From that day in September 2009, Victoria has continued to attend the Adventist Church.

On Sabbath, December 26, 2009, as a result of the Holy Spirit speaking to her heart, Victoria sealed her decision to follow Jesus by being baptized—a perfect Christmas present! Following her baptism, she continued studying the Discover Bible guides, completing the course in mid-2010 to become the one-millionth graduate of the Voice of Prophecy Bible School in North America! Today, Victoria describes how her decision to become a Seventh-day Adventist Christian has affected her life: "I now have a peace in my life, a calmness, that God has given me. God has removed the fear I had of talking to others about Him. Now I can pray with people and openly talk about my beliefs. My desire is to share Jesus with others."

The China Story

Kurt Johnson

The year was 1947. The Voice of Prophecy Bible School had been circling the globe for four years, when God placed the vision for such a school in the heart of Pastor David Lin and his colleagues in China. Pastor Lin translated the Voice of Prophecy English Bible guides, adapted them for the Chinese culture, and assisted in establishing a Bible correspondence school in Shanghai.

A young teacher became one of the early Bible course students in China. He needed some medicine and sent his little boy to the drugstore for the purchase. When his son returned, his father saw that the druggist had wrapped a piece of printed paper around the bottle of medicine. It was a *Voice of Prophecy* radio log, and it also advertised a free Bible correspondence course. Sometime before this, the young father had read about this same course in a copy of the Chinese *Signs of the Times*®, and now his interest was reawakened as he scrutinized the radio log.

He enrolled immediately and soon began poring over God's Word. After completing the series of lessons, the young man committed his life to Jesus. He became an enthusiastic supporter of the *Voice of Prophecy* broadcast and a passionate soul winner for Jesus, introducing hundreds of people to Jesus and enrolling them in the Bible course.

Shortly thereafter, in 1949, the Chinese Bible correspondence school was closed. But in 2005, God placed a burden for Bible schools in China on the heart of the Voice of Prophecy Bible School director, Kurt Johnson. Kurt shared his vision for Bible school work with other leaders in Asia and found that they, too, wanted as many Chinese people as possible—in China and worldwide—to be able to study God's Word.

People began praying, planning, and seeking God's leading. Local Chinese church leaders led the way. Today, there are numerous local church-based Bible study ministries in Chinese churches following the Discover Bible School concept. The first Discover Bible School was established in eastern China in 2007. Individuals attending local churches receive an opportunity not only to worship God and participate in other meetings and services, but to begin a study of God's Word using various Bible study guides. The Discover Guides and KidZone Bible lessons were translated into Traditional and Simplified Chinese and are being used to guide men and women, and boys and girls in a study of the Bible.

Today, the Word of God is a light shining upon the daily lives of billions of people living in Asia who are seeking the hope, love, and security that are found only in the Bible.

One Card, One Boy

Falvo Fowler

John watched intently as his favorite teacher talked with a tall stranger at the door of his classroom. The more the stranger talked, the more agitated John's teacher became. The conversation came to a sudden stop when the man offered John's teacher a card. In response, the teacher took the card, tore it up, and tossed the pieces in the trash! At this point, the stranger quietly turned and walked away.

With his curiosity piqued, John, together with a friend, went through the trash after class and retrieved the torn pieces. What had so upset their teacher? Using cooked rice as paste, they stuck the torn card back together. Then the reason for the teacher's agitation became clear. The card offered a Bible course that would answer three questions: (1) Is there a God? (2) Why is there suffering? (3) And is there life after death? John knew that his teacher was an atheist, and nothing offends an atheist so much as the promise to answer such profound questions. John, on the other hand, was very interested in the answers to these questions. So he wrote to the address on the card, asking for the Bible lessons it offered.

The Voice of Prophecy office in Pune, India, wrote back to John, saying that he was too young to take the lessons.

But John was not put off so easily. He wrote again, asking, "If I'm old enough to write for the lessons, aren't I old enough to take them?"

Apparently, a person in the Voice of Prophecy office agreed. John and his friend received the lessons, and they carefully studied and worked through every lesson until they had completed the course.

About this time, Pastor D. S. David arrived in John's town—a town of gold miners and machinists—to conduct an evangelistic series. John was one of his first contacts. The series of meetings lasted three weeks. The following year Pastor David held meetings in this town for three months. John attended every meeting even though this meant sometimes walking alone several miles each way in the dark. John made it a point to learn more about Scripture. The meetings followed up on what he had learned from the Voice of Prophecy course and built on that early introduction to truth.

At the end of this second series of meetings, John asked to be baptized, but Pastor David wanted to make sure this son of the Anglican faith would stay true to the fundamental teaching of the Bible Sabbath. When the second portion of a two-part final government exam fell on the Sabbath, John and his friend had a choice to make. *Would they sit for the exam on Sabbath or not?* John's friend chose to write the exam although it took place on the Sabbath. John's father encouraged him to go ahead and write the exam on the Sabbath. "Imagine," he said to John, "how many more people you can minister to as a doctor if you write the exam and get a high grade. God will understand." But, for John, the Sabbath he had learned about in the Voice of Prophecy lessons—the Sabbath that Pastor David had challenged him to keep— was more important than his dream of becoming a doctor.

His score on the first part of the two-part exam was high enough to carry him through—even without taking the second part that was held on the Sabbath! His "First Class" marks on the exam qualified him for a scholarship to go to any professional school in his state—medicine, engineering, or any other field of study. But the tug of Bible truth and the influence of that winsome evangelist Pastor David led John to enter

Spicer Memorial College and study to obtain a degree in religion.

A couple of years after graduation from Spicer Memorial College, John married Mary—the sister of Pastor David!

John's choices—to take the Voice of Prophecy Bible lessons, to keep the Sabbath, and to become a minister—took that young boy from the poverty in which he had grown up to college and then to a master's degree in theology and journalism, and eventually a doctorate at Andrews University. He went on to become the first Indian editor-in-chief of the Oriental Watchman Publishing House, then the leading Adventist publishing house serving Asia and Africa. John was the first Indian educational director of the Southern Asia Division and the first to be called to the General Conference.

The Voice of Prophecy Bible course card, discarded by his atheist teacher, led John Fowler to a global journey in ministry. Through the years, he has expanded and shared, in his preaching and writing (books, periodicals, articles, etc.), the early Bible education he received through the Voice of Prophecy Bible course. John has retired officially after fifty-two years of service, but continues serving in ministry. His life is proof that when a person chooses to believe and then chooses to act on that belief, God does wonders. Miracles happen; sometimes not immediately, but they do happen.

One card. One boy. And the multitudes continue to be fed spiritually.

※

Falvo Fowler is the son of John and Mary Fowler and the father of Mikailyn Fowler. He is an editor in the General Conference Sabbath School and Personal Ministries Department and also produces media/apps for the department.

Dumpster Evangelism

Trash Cans, Pianos, and Frozen Radio Dials

Kurt Johnson

Over the years I have marveled at the ways God uses simple Bible study enrollment cards offering free Bible lessons to bring people into a relationship with Him. In this chapter, I will be sharing with you several short stories of God's miraculous leading in the lives of individuals. These stories tell me that no one can *quench the endless means* by which God reaches out to His children who need to find Him and His truth for today.

Card in a Trash Can Leads to Baptism

I don't recommend throwing Bible study enrollment cards or religious literature in the garbage can, but if they end up there, God can still use them!

Fred was visiting his daughter in the state of Virginia. One morning, as Fred was leaving her apartment, he noticed that the garbage can in her kitchen was full. So he carried the garbage sack outside to the dumpster that serves his daughter's apartment building. When Fred opened the lid, he noticed a number of cards lying in the dumpster on top of the bags of trash. He picked one up. It was a Voice of Prophecy Discover Bible School enrollment card.

The local Adventist Church, under the leadership of Pastor Bob Parrish, had recently blanketed their community area with a mass distribution of the enrollment cards. Some residents of the apartment complex apparently were not interested in Bible studies, so they threw the cards away. But God is still in control of the lives of people.

Fred took the Discover enrollment card home and filled out the information. "Right then," he says, "I started on a new road to the true worship of Jesus." Fred was a diligent student and soon finished the course. He says he found the treasure of truth from the Bible. Fred called the local Adventist church to find the address and began attending services. After a review of the lessons he had studied, Fred was baptized.

God uses every possible means to lead people into a relationship with Him and eternal life—even a card thrown away in a dumpster! Never give up. Never get discouraged. Keep sharing and witnessing—and God will bring a harvest!

"Dear God, I Need a Bible"

Howard was collecting cans to recycle from dumpsters behind grocery stores in the Lexington, Kentucky, area. One day while Howard was rummaging through a dumpster, he came across a Discover Bible Guide that someone had thrown away. Howard picked it up, looked it over, and told his wife that he was going to take it home. "All we need now," he told her, "is a Bible. Maybe we can find a Bible to go along with the lesson!"

You guessed it! A few days later, Howard found a Bible—in a dumpster! With the help of his newfound "dumpster Bible," Howard completed the "dumpster study guide" and mailed it to the address of the local Discover Bible School that was stamped on the answer sheet. The local Discover School corrected the answer sheet and sent lesson 1 to get Howard started on the entire set of Discover guides.

After lesson 9, the local church contacted Howard and invited him to attend church. He came and soon accepted Jesus as his Savior and the Lord of his life, anchoring his decision in baptism.

I love Howard's story. It appears that someone was so upset with God that he or she threw away the Bible guide. Then someone else threw a Bible in a dumpster; it may have been their way of rejecting God. But in the process that person unwittingly became an evangelist and brought Howard to the foot of the cross!

A Frozen Radio Dial

I was participating in a Voice of Prophecy rally near Dallas, Texas. During Sabbath School we highlighted the history of the Voice of Prophecy Bible School. Afterward, I met a Discover Bible School student who shared the following story with me. I'll call the student "Mary."

Mary had a weekly ritual. Every Sunday evening she sat down at her writing desk, took out paper and pen, and turned on her radio. She never changed the dial, because Mary had a favorite program, and this was all she ever listened to. So she left the dial in place. As she listened to her program, she wrote letters to friends and family. This was her weekly time to relax and stay connected.

One particular Sunday evening, Mary got out her writing materials as usual and turned on her radio. However, there was a problem. Instead of her favorite program, another program was playing. Mary heard the words, "Lift up the trumpet, and loud let it ring: Jesus is coming again!" In frustration she looked at her radio dial. Had it moved? If so, how? She hadn't changed it.

Mary reached out and tried to turn the dial and find her usual program. But to her frustration, the dial would not move! She twisted it as hard as she could, but to no avail. The dial simply would not budge! After numerous attempts, Mary finally gave up. Puzzled and upset, she began writing notes to her friends while the new program continued.

She didn't know it, but she was listening to the thirty-minute, Sunday-evening broadcast of the Voice of Prophecy. After the introductions and music, Pastor Lonnie Melashenko, speaker-director of the Voice of Prophecy, began sharing his message. After a few minutes, Mary laid down her pen. She stopped writing and began listening intently to the message. The Holy Spirit was speaking to her heart, and when the announcer offered free Discover Bible guides at the end of the broadcast, Mary wrote down the address.

This began her journey in Bible study. Soon Mary was preparing for baptism. The interesting part of the story? The next Sunday night, her radio dial was no longer frozen, and her old favorite program came on as it always did!

An Amazing Piano Story

Some stories become legends as God leads in such an obvious and amazing way that the story is passed on from decade to decade. At a meeting of Bible school leaders from around the world, Mike Strickland and Martin Anthony, Bible school leaders from Great Britain, shared the following story with me.

In 1955, an Adventist church member from West London went door-to-door in Watford, handing out cards offering free Bible studies. One homeowner took the card. At some point (no one knows when) he must have thought, *I can use this to fix the vibration in that panel at the back of my piano!* He folded the card several times, making a thick wedge. Then he removed a screw from the vibrating panel, inserted the folded card between the panel and the piano, and replaced the screw, running it right through the card.

Twenty-five years later, in 1980, the piano was sold to a local woman. She played the piano for several months and then called a piano tuner to come to her home and tune the instrument. In the course of his work, the piano tuner removed the panel, noticing that someone had folded up a card to wedge between the panel and the back of the piano. He unfolded the card, laid it on top of the piano, and completed his work.

After he left, the new owner saw the card lying on her piano. Although it had been folded repeatedly and had a hole through it, she was still able to read it after twenty-five years. She decided she would like to take advantage of the Bible lessons the card offered. She didn't know how long the card had been wedged in the piano panel, but she decided to write and see what happened. She sat down and wrote a note to the Voice of Prophecy Bible School, enclosed the damaged card and the note in an envelope, and mailed it to the Bible School in Watford at the address on the card.

A few days later, the first Bible lesson appeared in her mailbox! The lady and her daughter studied the lessons. Later, her daughter enrolled at the Adventist school in Stanborough Park, becoming the "head girl" in her senior year. Both mother and daughter became baptized members of the local Seventh-day Adventist church.

Mike Strickland said as he shared the story, "I still have that folded, damaged card in my files at the Bible school. In fact, I often carry it to churches on Sabbath to show our church members and encourage them to be faithful in distributing Bible school enrollment cards. Even when no results are immediately apparent, you never know what will happen at some point!"

As I share these stories, I am reminded from Scripture that if God can talk through a donkey and "even the stones cry out," never underestimate the means He will use for the salvation of people living in our neighborhoods and communities. Garbage cans and pianos become God's evangelists. He can use you and me through simple means—being a friend to a neighbor or someone at work may lead to someone's salvation. Putting an enrollment card offering free Bible studies in a birthday card or on someone's door or including it with a telephone bill when you pay it or leaving the card with your tip in a restaurant or in the pocket of the seat on an airplane or—use your imagination—it may be the means of someone's eternal salvation. Go ahead and try it. If God can use a trash can, I am sure He can use you and me!

Fordyce W. Detamore

The Man Who Launched the Voice of Prophecy Bible School

Kurt Johnson

W hen Fordyce Detamore was seven years old, he wrote a letter to his father telling him that he had decided to be a preacher. He never wavered from that conviction and grew up with a heart for evangelism. For thirty-five years, Fordyce lived out of suitcases on the evangelistic trail as well as serving in a number of other functions and positions in ministry.

Early in his evangelistic career, Fordyce began using a roving microphone so he wouldn't be tied to one position but could stride up and down the entire platform. Someone sitting behind him would reel the cord in or out as the situation demanded. One night in Kansas City, Missouri, a young child sitting in the front row was listening and watching the preacher very intently. Pastor Detamore, preaching enthusiastically, made a quick turn and walked back across the platform, stretching the cord out behind him. The little boy turned to his mother and declared in a voice loud enough for everyone to hear, "Look, Mother, that dummy runs by electricity!"

Fordyce was, indeed, a living dynamo. He spoke fast. He walked fast. He accomplished more in twenty-four hours than most men. When I was a young pastor studying at the seminary in Berrien Springs, Michigan, Pastor Detamore conducted an evangelistic series at the Village Church nearby. I had heard about Fordyce and his enthusiastic preaching style, so I attended the meetings to witness it firsthand. That was an inspiration to me. Pastor Detamore was known not only for being a dynamic, enthusiastic preacher, but for his heart-felt visitation and his skill at bringing people to make a decision for Jesus. Pastor Detamore's initials were F. W. D. (Fordyce William Detamore), which also stand for "four-wheel drive" in reference to vehicles. Some of Fordyce's friends suggested this described Fordyce perfectly. He was always "geared up," going forward for God!

Fordyce is known as the man who began the Voice of Prophecy Bible Correspondence School. Here is the story. About 1937, Fordyce and his wife, Aletha, were pastoring the St. Louis, Missouri, Seventh-day Adventist Church. Before beginning this pastorate, Pastor Detamore had gone to Philadelphia and assisted evangelist John Ford with a series of meetings. John Ford had been trained by Charles T. Everson, a well-known, successful evangelist in the early decades of the twentieth century. While working with Pastor Ford, Fordyce learned a complete plan of evangelism, which combined strong personal work with public evangelism.

Returning to St. Louis, Pastor Detamore incorporated his newly learned techniques to increase decisions for Jesus and the truths of Scripture. He named his meeting place "The Bible Auditorium." He also applied a principle he learned by observing H. M. S. Richards of the Voice of Prophecy—he started a local radio program, calling it "The Bible Auditorium of the Air." Linking the radio program with the physical meeting place increased attendance at his meetings.

Around 1940, Fordyce was attending an evangelism institute in Boulder, Colorado, taught by Pastor J. L. Shuler. One day, Shuler mentioned a pastor who because he did not have an evangelistic budget had started a local Bible correspondence course instead. Something clicked in Fordyce's mind. He jumped to his feet and asked, "Wouldn't such a Bible course be an excellent way to follow up radio interests?" Pastor Shuler agreed that this was an excellent idea.

Within two weeks Detamore began offering free Bible lessons by mail on his local radio program in Kansas City. Immediately, he received 150 requests, and by year end, some two thousand individuals were studying the lessons through the mail! A retired Bible instructor corrected the lessons.

When the bombing of Pearl Harbor took place on December 7, 1941, Fordyce, Aletha, and their children were getting settled in Glendale, California, where Fordyce was now the announcer for the *Voice of Prophecy* radio broadcast. It was in this atmosphere of uncertainty in America that the Voice of Prophecy expanded its range and went coast-to-coast on the Mutual Broadcasting Network. And it was Fordyce's voice that gave the greeting, "Hello America!" Fordyce soon approached Pastor H. M. S. Richards with the request to begin a correspondence school for the radio program. Pastor Richards agreed to give it a try.

On Sunday evening, February 1, 1942, Fordyce announced the Bible School of the Air and offered Bible lessons by mail! It was an idea that caught on like wildfire. Today, some seventy years later, the Voice of Prophecy Bible School has expanded to include the Internet, cell phones, and other new technologies, along with the printed correspondence lessons. But the principle is the same—providing a way of studying the Bible to introduce individuals around the world to a relationship with Jesus and the truth of the Scriptures.

Bessie Detamore, Fordyce's mother, assisted with the Bible school and contributed much to its success. For twenty-five years she dictated letters, answering questions raised by students, and assisted with the organizational operation of the Bible school. Those who were part of the Voice of Prophecy ministry in those days have shared with me that although Fordyce launched the Bible school, Bessie was the one that made sure the day-to-day operation was successful.

Before we leave this chapter, I want to share a miracle story that occurred while Fordyce and Aletha were serving in Borneo as the acting director of the Borneo Mission in the 1930s. On one occasion, Fordyce and Pastor Youngberg made a trip up the Tatau River to locate a new mission site. They came to an area that looked promising, but upon exploring, they discovered bodies placed in trees, an indication that this was sacred ground, so they continued with their journey.

As the day wore on and they decided to beach their canoe for lunch, they kept finding fresh crocodile tracks wherever they tried to stop. So lunch had to take place in the canoe. Arriving at one village, they found a typical family longhouse in a small clearing in the woods. A basket of human skulls above the door was a telltale sign that these people were headhunters. Nevertheless, the two pastors were welcomed. Upon entering the thatched house, they met the grandmother who was the "witch doctor" for the village. They visited with the family and shared with them about Jesus and His love for them. Before leaving, the two men taught the family a simple prayer.

Several months later, the pastors returned to this village, and the people there told them the story of a little girl who had become lost in the jungle. Knowing she would be surrounded by scorpions, highly poisonous snakes that dropped from trees, and wild animals, the villagers did not expect her to survive if she had to spend the night there in the jungle. Search parties hunted for the little girl, but to no avail. Then the searchers remembered the prayer they had recently learned from the two missionaries. Deciding to put it to the test, the villagers prayed the simple prayer to the God of heaven. In the early hours of the morning, the family heard the little girl calling them to let her into the house. With tears of joy, they listened as the little girl told them that she, too, had prayed the white man's prayer while lost in the jungle. When she finished praying, she said she saw a large man dressed in white and wearing a white *topi,* or pith helmet, that the missionaries wore in those tropical countries. The man was very kind. He took her by the hand and led her through the jungle right up to her own longhouse!

The entire family—witch doctor and all—accepted the love of Jesus, for they had learned that the angels of the Lord surround those who trust and love Him.

This story exemplifies Fordyce Detamore's ministry—a man who at his death was known as a "human dynamo" for God. Pastor Detamore died on May 15, 1980, while living in Portland, Oregon, but his influence and legacy still lives in the Voice of Prophecy Bible School!

℧

This chapter, written by Kurt Johnson, was adapted from *God's Living Dynamo: The Story of Fordyce W. Detamore,* by Arlene Detamore Dever. This book and biographical information were provided by Homer Dever, son-in-law of Fordyce who was married to Fordyce's daughter, Arlene Detamore; and from Fordyce's granddaughter Ronda Dever.

Note From Kurt Johnson:

I had the honor and unique pleasure of talking with Homer Dever before his death in 2012. In a unique set of circumstances Homer studied the Voice of Prophecy Bible courses as a young man, which had a part in Homer becoming a Seventh-day Adventist. One of his diplomas is displayed in the pictorial section of this book signed in 1943 by Fordyce Detamore and H. M. S. Richards. Homer married Arlene

Detamore in 1955, and Fordyce became the father-in-law of the man he helped spiritually through the Bible school! After being married for more than fifty years, both Arlene and Homer have fallen asleep in Jesus, now waiting for His soon return.

H. M. S. Richards Sr.

On the Air Every Day, Everywhere

Kurt Johnson

The year H. M. S. Richards (1894–1985) was born, Guglielmo Marconi discovered that he could send messages through the air without wires! Though he received little encouragement in his native Italy, Marconi was convinced that his discoveries could lead to a new system of communication.

Sailing to England, he found individuals who took an interest in what he was developing. Soon he was filing for a patent and demonstrating his invention to all who would listen and watch. When Marconi succeeded in sending a signal across the Atlantic from Cornwall, England, to St. John's, Newfoundland, Harold Richards was a preschool boy playing on his grandfather's Colorado farm.

Radio continued to grow, and so did young Harold Richards. While he was dating a young schoolteacher, Mabel Eastman, in Ottawa, Canada, the first commercial radio broadcasting station in America was being developed in Pittsburgh, Pennsylvania. On November 2, 1920, operating on a frequency of 833kc with fifty watts of power, KDKA went on the air with the returns of the Harding-Cox presidential election. The next ten years, from 1920 to 1930, saw the radio broadcasting industry explode with dynamic activity.

Soon after arriving in California as an evangelist, H. M. S. Richards began to think about the potential of radio. He would look out over the crowds that came to his tent meetings and think, "If only I could preach on the radio, I could reach thousands of people with the gospel where now I am reaching only hundreds."

Before we complete the story, let's go back to the beginning.

Harold Marshall Sylvester Richards was born in the little town of Davis, Iowa. His father was a preacher, and his mother played the piano for their evangelistic tent meetings. Harold's mother and father had met in a tent; his father had proposed in a tent; and little Harold came close to being born in a tent! His mother made it home just in time for his birth.

As Harold was growing up, his parents would bring him to the tent for the meetings, leaving him in a crib on the back seat of the auditorium. He grew up with the smell of canvas in his nostrils. He learned that a tent must be stretched tight, but not too tight. That a tent wet from the rain needed to be loosened so the wet canvas could shrink. Tent meetings were his heritage.

When Harold was a toddler, he once got into the backyard and ate so many green apples that he literally became deathly ill. The doctor said there was little he could do so Harold's mother prayed, dedicating her little boy to God and His service—and the toddler was healed!

Harold spent most of his growing up years near Loveland, Colorado, where his grandparents, Two-Moms and Two-Pops, lived. When he was ten years old, he experienced a tragedy that could have ended his life. His life was spared, but his eyesight was damaged permanently. Here's what happened.

His father had been away preaching a six-week series of gospel messages, but was due home at any time. Harold and his brother Kenneth were exploring an irrigation ditch when they found the barrel of an old shotgun buried in the mud. It looked, to them, like a cannon! They had been repeatedly warned about guns and gunpowder, but they were curious boys, and the most pressing thing suddenly became "Where can we find some gunpowder to fire our cannon?" A neighbor boy furnished them with some of his father's blasting powder in exchange for a ringside seat at the event.

The powder was in grains about the size of small peas. They carefully loaded the rusty gun barrel with about three inches of blasting powder, added some small rocks, a few old nails, and some wads of paper until the barrel was packed full. Then the boys hauled their prize to a spot in the barnyard, fastened it to a log with baling wire, and aimed it at some unsuspecting pigeons on the nearby barn roof.

Harold stooped and squinted along the barrel of the gun. "Perfect!" he proclaimed. "Now, get out of the way!" Just as he was starting to insert a fuse into the touchhole, he heard someone coming up the lane. It was his father returning from his trip! Harold made a split-second decision. Instead of taking the necessary time to insert a fuse and then light it, he simply struck a match and shoved the burning end into the open touchhole.

A loud *boom* sent wads of paper, nails, rocks and powder out the gun barrel and touchhole in a huge explosion. It also sent a frightened, injured boy to the country doctor as fast as Old Nell could pull the wagon. After the wounds healed, Harold found that he could see only a small amount of light with his left eye and that he had a noticeable weakness and nearsightedness in his right. However, the accident did not deter his reading. He discovered that he could read with one eye almost as well as with two. Later in life he wore thick glasses to enable him to read.

An Adventist academy was established in Loveland, Colorado, during this time, and its first graduating class had only a single graduate—Harold Richards. He went on to attend Washington Missionary College (now Washington Adventist University), near Washington, D.C., where he stoked furnaces at night and studied during the day until he earned his batchelor's degree. In the summers, he and his friend Kenneth Gant would preach at tent meetings.

Following graduation, Pastor Richards accepted a call to pastor a small church in Toronto, Ontario, Canada. The church school teacher there was Mabel Eastman. Soon Pastor Richards was stopping by the grade school daily to make sure that the teacher and students were getting along OK. Harold and Mabel were married on April 14, 1920, in the little town of Harmony Corners, Ontario.

Before long, Harold and Mabel moved to Southern California, where he served as an evangelist. Up and down the state he went—Lodi, Hanford, Shafter, Bakersfield, Sacramento, Chico, Fresno, Long Beach, Inglewood, Merced, Visalia—preaching God's Word. In some cities he built huge wooden "tabernacles." In others he pitched two large three-pole tents side-by-side to accommodate the crowds. He baptized thousands of people.

These series of meetings were long and strenuous. It was common for Harold to preach seven nights a week for six months at a time! At the end of the series, sometimes a new church would be started. In other cases, the existing church received a large influx of new members.

Then came radio . . . and we return to the story where we left off a few paragraphs above.

Back in the late 1920s the idea of preaching on the radio was a new concept. Some who thought they "knew all about these things" scoffed at Richards' dream of preaching on the radio. "You can't expect to do any good preaching on the radio," they told him. "Nobody has ever done it. Besides, it would cost too much money. Who'd pay for it?"

But Pastor Richards kept talking and dreaming about preaching on the radio. He prayed about it and really felt that God wanted him to take this step. One day on a camping trip with two of his friends, Harold Young and Glenn Luther, the men turned to Richards and said, "Harold, you say that you think God wants you to be on the radio."

"That's right," he replied.

"You don't believe any such thing."

"Why, yes I do!"

"No, we don't believe you do."

"Why don't you believe it?"

"Well," they said, "if you believed—if you really believed—that God wants you on the radio, and if you are willing to go on the radio, then you'd be on the radio."

Pastor Richards couldn't argue with their logic, so the next time he stood up to preach, he told his tent audience that he was going on the radio. He was already using all the evening offerings to help pay for his tent meetings, so he proposed that the next night everyone bring in old jewelry to get the radio work started. Items began to pour in—old watches, wedding rings, bracelets, eyeglass frames, even gold teeth! When all the items were sold, the results totaled two hundred dollars. That was the beginning of the radio ministry. Richards' suit pocket became the collecting place for items for the radio ministry. Soon Pastor Richards was on the radio every day. First it was fifteen-minute devotionals on KNX in Los Angeles. Later he put the entire evangelistic meeting on the air for an hour each night.

Then the radio mail began to pour in. At first, Pastor Richards attempted to answer the letters himself, but it was impossible. After a week, a woman by the name of Betty Cannon offered her services as secretary. An unused chicken coop in the Richards' backyard was set up for Betty's office. The agreement was that Betty would be paid whenever funds came in the mail that would cover her costs. Miraculously, God provided, and there was always just enough money coming in to pay the radio expenses.

Destiny has strange ways of accomplishing its ends. A singing quartet, "The Lone Star Four," from the state of Texas, three of them brothers, headed to California to study nursing at St. Helena. The year was 1935, and the quartet wanted to stay together and sing, so they chose nursing as a vocation to provide their means of support. The three brothers were Waldo, Wesley, and Lewis Crane, along with Ray Turner, bass.

H. M. S. Richards was speaking at the Glendale Sanitarium when he heard the Lone Star Four sing. He arranged for the quartet to sing for his meetings in Long Beach—an event that would change all of their lives forever. Pastor Richards quickly decided that he wanted the quartet to work full time for his radio and evangelism ministry. It took some efforts to arrange funding, but before long the Lone Star Four signed on to become a part of the ministry at a salary of thirty dollars per month.

The Lone Star Four and H.M.S. Richards

At this time, the radio program was known as "The Bible Tabernacle of the Air." However, when the program began to be carried on an eighteen-station network (Don Lee Broadcasting System) on the West Coast in 1937, a contest was held to rename it. As a result, the broadcast became the *Voice of Prophecy.* At the same time, the Lone Star Four became the King's Heralds.

On Sunday evening, January 4, 1942, the broadcast was beamed coast-to-coast on the eighty-nine-station Mutual Broadcasting System. Those in the studio for the memorable event were H. M. S. Richards, speaker; the King's Heralds (then composed of George Casebeer, Bob Seamount, Wesley Crane, and Ray Turner); Fordyce Detamore, announcer; and Elmer Digneo, organist. When the red broadcasting light flashed on, the words to the song, "Lift up the trumpet, and loud let it ring: Jesus is coming again!" rang out for the first time nationwide over the airwaves!

But most important of all was the fact that lives were being saved for eternity. The response was tremendous. During the month of October 1942, the broadcast received 22,711 letters from radio listeners! The radio audience was taking the program to heart and supporting the ministry financially.

In 1947, the Voice of Prophecy invited Del Delker to join the music group as contralto soloist. Her full, rich voice was an immediate success with the radio audience. Del's kind, humble personality and her love for people and for Jesus formed a bond between her and tens of thousands around the world. One of her first songs, "The Love of God," became Del's theme song for many years.

Del was born in Java, South Dakota, and began to sing almost as soon as she could talk. One day, three-year-old Del wandered away from home. When her frantic mother finally located her, the little girl was singing on a street corner, her fist full of coins which passersby had given her!

When Del was a small girl the family moved to Oakland, California. Del was brought up in a Christian home, but as a teenager she drifted away from her walk with God. Through the ministry of the Quiet Hour and J. L. Tucker, she was led to recommit her life to God. She then began to sing on *The Quiet Hour* radio broadcast. When she received the call to join the Voice of Prophecy, Del struggled with the decision. But when she said "Yes," the peace she experienced told her that this was God's plan for her life.

Del has been—and continues to be—a real witness for Jesus through her music ministry. Today, many are blessed by her recordings. Del's passion is for Jesus to come soon, and her desire is that God will have used her ministry to lead many to an eternal walk with Him.

Today, the *Voice of Prophecy* radio ministry and the Bible School are still reaching lives. Yes, the technology and delivery formats have changed significantly from those early days of radio, but one thing has not changed over the past eighty-plus years—preparing the people of the world for the soon return of Jesus Christ.

As H. M. S. Richards always said at the end of each of his broadcasts: "Keep looking up, going forward in faith. Have faith, dear friend, in God."

જી

Adapted from A Voice in the Air, *by Robert E. Edwards and from* H. M. S. Richards: Man Alive! *by Virginia Cason (adaptation by Kurt Johnson).*

List of Bible-School Directors and Supervisors

1942–1944	Fordyce Detamore, founder, director
1949–1972	Bernice Davidson, supervisor
1969–1972	Dan Guild, director
1972–1975	Clarence Gruesbeck, director
1976–1978	Elden Walter, director
1980–1982	Bonnie Atherton, supervisor
1982–1984	Leilani Proctor, supervisor, Bible School coordinator
1984–1988	Arlys Qualley, Bible School coordinator
1988–1990	Ilene Diede, supervisor
1991–1995	Lina Sanchez, supervisor
1995–1997	Jan Judd, supervisor
1997–2004	Calvin Smith, associate director
1997–present	Mariel Swenson, associate director
1997–present	Kurt Johnson, director

Photo Gallery

LESSON TWO

CREATION OR EVOLUTION?

KEY TEXT: In the beginning God created the heaven and the earth. — Genesis 1:1.

BY THE inroads of the theory of evolution an attack is being made on the Word of God and on the sovereignty of the Creator. Some are believers in evolution *without* God; others claim to believe in evolution *and* God. Evolution is being taught to the younger pupils as well as the advanced students in schools throughout the land. Recent surveys show that over 40 per cent of the ministers of the United States believe in evolution. Many sample surveys show a percentage as high as sixty-five out of every hundred of the clergy accepting evolution. Taking the more conservative figure, it means that approximately 60,000 ministers in the sacred desk today believe evolution in preference to the Bible record of creation.

Is it any wonder that recent years have witnessed such an immense increase in the number of atheists and agnostics? In order that you may be more firmly established in your faith in the Bible, and that you may have evidences with which to combat the evil influences rampant today, let us review creation and examine evolution.

EARTH'S ORIGIN

1 What simple statement of fundamental fact introduces God's Holy Word?

In the beginning God created the heaven and the earth.—Genesis 1:1.

All the rest of the Bible hinges on the acceptance or rejection of that essential and basic truth, "God created the heaven and the earth." That is the Bible claim of man's true origin. *To create* means to make something out of nothing. Man cannot do that; and, because he is incapable of performing an act of creation, in his pride man is often loathe to credit his Maker with that power.

FAITH ESTABLISHED THROUGH EVIDENCES IN GOD'S CREATED WORKS

2 How only can we understand the mystery of Creation?

THROUGH FAITH we understand that the worlds were framed by the word of God, so that things which are seen were not made of things which do appear. . . . But WITHOUT FAITH it is IMPOSSIBLE to please him: for he that cometh to God must believe that he is. and that he is a rewarder of them that diligently seek him. — Hebrews 11:3,6.

The Apostle states clearly that one must *have faith* to accept the mystery of creation. But he adds that those who diligently seek God will find a reward and satisfaction in their faith. Even as a child must accept by faith the story of his parentage, so *we* must accept by faith from our heavenly Father the story of *our* origin.

Some claim a very profound regard for logic and scientific data by demanding concrete proof for *everything*; what cannot be materially proved they discard. Yet they fail to recognize that they manifest faith daily in their fellow men. Faith in others is the cement which holds together the whole structure of society. Paul says faith is essential also to all spiritual comprehension.

Men have faith in the baker; they believe the bread is not poisoned. Men have faith in train schedules; else they would not go down to meet a train, for the report of a train arrival is only hearsay. Men go to work daily, *believing* that they will receive wages at the end of the month. All business transactions hinge on faith. Men do not understand electricity, yet they have faith to believe in God that it takes to turn the light switch when you enter a dark room. God is near you now, and if you will just switch from unbelief to simple belief, He will become apparent to you through His created works. (Lesson 6,

"How to Overcome Doubt," will be a help in establishing faith.)

3 To what does all nature testify?

The heavens DECLARE THE GLORY OF GOD: and the firmament SHEWETH HIS HANDYWORK. . . . There is no speech nor language, where their voice is not heard.—Psalm 19:1, 3.

When I consider thy heavens. the work of thy fingers. the moon and the stars. which thou hast ordained: what is man. that thou art mindful of him?—Psalm 8: 3, 4.

In addition to life on this earth, God created the sun, moon, stars, and other planets. Look up at the stars at night. They shine to the glory of their Creator. There is no land so dark in sin or ignorance but that it has the testimony of the stars that there is a God. The scientific wonders of nature *all* testify that there is a great mind back of all the details of plant and animal life, as well as in the atomic structure of the inanimate.

Who would be so foolish as to claim that a watch came into existence by accidental processes; that an automobile just happened; that a printing press is the result of thousands or millions of years of self-adjusted evolving? If we admit that all manufactured articles must have a designer and maker, is it not reasonable to believe that this world, its life, and its people, likewise had a Designer and Maker?

The noted astronomer, Dr. J. H. Jeans, stated after years of analytical study of the universe: "Everything points with overwhelming force to a definite event, or series of events of creation at some time or times, not infinitely remote. The universe cannot have originated by chance out of its present ingredients."—*Eos, or the Wider Aspects of Cosmogony,* page 55.

The great Designer and Maker of the universe—the Originator—we call *God.*

The first Voice of Prophecy worldwide Bible correspondence full doctrinal course, circa 1942.

Box 55	Los Angeles 53, California	Lesson 12

SCIENCE, BIBLE, AND GOD

A SHIP'S LIBRARIAN, on receiving a package of "eats" from home, tried to hide his treasure where the other sailors would not find it. Opening a seldom-used cabinet in the library, he found fifty dusty Bibles on whose flyleaves was written, "Gift to the training ship *St. Mary* from the Bible Society." The books apparently had never been opened since they were placed on the ship. One by one, he tossed them out the porthole, planning to store his gift package where they had been kept. Just as he closed the cabinet door, smiling to himself because of his bright idea, a voice boomed down the hatchway, "What's going on down there?"

"Nothing, Captain. Why?" he called out innocently.

"Come up on deck and see why!" commanded the officer.

The sailor hurried up the hatchway and peered over the ship's side. To his surprise, he saw a veritable fleet of Bibles floating about ten yards apart in a beautiful, slow-moving arc. All that the guilty librarian could mumble in reply to the angry captain was, "I'm sorry, Captain. I thought they would sink."

The atheist, infidel, agnostic, materialist, and higher critic have deluded themselves into thinking that same thought. But, friend, the Word of God will never sink. It has stood the test of ages of attack from many quarters. Remember the poem in our first lesson, "The Anvil of God's Word"? Another poem says:

> All efforts to destroy are vain—
> God's Holy Word will still remain;
> So hammer on, ye hostile hands,
> Your hammers break, God's anvil stands.

1 HAS SCIENCE EXPLODED THE BOOK?

Enemies of the Bible have made numerous false charges against it as they have tried to prove it to be unscientific. The simple reading of the Book will readily convince the unbiased that it makes no statement which, upon investigation, can be proved contrary to demonstrated scientific fact. The difficulty is that many of the ideas held by churchmen of the Dark Ages are *supposed to have been taken from the Bible*. The unbelieving critic reads of the fantastic teachings of the wise men of past centuries and blames the Bible for these false notions. Would he but read the Bible from cover to cover for himself, he would soon discover that the false suppositions of the ancients never came from that Holy Book.

Fortunately for the Bible, it has often through the centuries been out of step with the beliefs of the sages of science. As research has advanced in quest of scientific fact, scientists have changed their minds so often that it would require more than a mental contortionist jump back and forth across the fence trying to keep in step with their changing ideas.

The word "science" means *to know*. But in many cases the things that science thought it knew a century

Being from the same source —

HOW COULD THEY FAIL TO HARMONIZE?

ago, it discards today. Had the Bible agreed with the science of medieval times, it would now be an exploded book. Had it harmonized with science even one hundred years ago, we should consider it outmoded in these enlightened times. But the Bible has never agreed with the false scientific theories of the past — science that grew out of the ignorance, suppositions, and superstitions of pagan times.

Compared with the Bible, science is an infant, still groping for fact. Dr. E. E. Slosson wrote in his book, *Sermons of a Chemist:*

The second full doctrinal course developed by the Voice of Prophecy was entitled "The Faith."

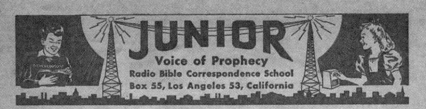

JUNIOR
Voice of Prophecy
Radio Bible Correspondence School
Box 55, Los Angeles 53, California

LESSON FIVE

HOW TO BE SAVED

MEMORY VERSE: Except ye be converted, and become as little children, ye shall not enter into the kingdom of heaven.—Matthew 18:3.

Thousands of Juniors are longing to know how they can be *sure* of being saved. In our memory verse Jesus explains that being converted, getting ready for heaven, is so simple that even a little child can understand it.

1 What is our great need in order that we will have a desire to turn from sin?

Speaking of the fearfulness of sin, Paul said:

O wretched man that I am! who shall deliver me from the body of this death?—Romans 7:24.

If one is to find his way to Jesus and salvation, he must first realize the awfulness of sin, feel his sinful condition and his need of help. Telling of his struggle with sin, Paul speaks of himself as "wretched." He compares the load of sin in one's life to dragging around a dead body.

Should you visit the museum in Athens, Greece, you would see a strange sight in one of the rear rooms—two bodies fastened close together by a heavy chain. The bodies and the chains have petrified and become like stone. You ask, "What has that to do with sin?" Long ago the courts sometimes sentenced a criminal to die by being chained to a dead man's body. Imagine how terrible that would be, to come to a slow horrible death, tied to a dead body. Those petrified bodies in the Athens museum had been chained together; a living man had been chained to a dead body. When he died, the two bodies were buried together. Sin is like that. If you stay tied to the sin-life, it will destroy your desire to do right and will finally cause you to be destroyed.

In order to be saved, you must cut loose from sin. If you admit that you need help to be free from your former wrong ways, then the Lord can save you.

BELIEF IN JESUS' SAVING POWER

2 What is the most important question in all the world, and what is its answer?

The keeper of the prison . . . came trembling . . . and said, Sirs, WHAT MUST I DO TO BE SAVED? And they said, BELIEVE on the Lord Jesus Christ, and thou shalt be saved.—Acts 16:27-31.

Here is a picture of a sinful jailer who suddenly felt his need of a Saviour. He was afraid that he would be lost, and in agony he cried out, "What must I do to be saved?" Jesus, our loving, merciful Saviour, never passes by a call like that.

Quickly Paul answered, "Believe on *Jesus* and you will be saved." Only *Jesus* can save.

REPENTANCE

3 What is the next step toward Jesus — toward being saved?

Repent ye therefore, and be converted, that your sins may be blotted out.—Acts 3:19.

Peter said to this group of people, whose hearts were longing for salvation, "Repent."

You ask, "But what does it mean to repent?" Repentance is simply turning from the old ways of sin. Sin leads to death. Remember, "the wages of sin is death." Rom. 6:23. When you decide to accept Jesus as your Saviour, you have a change of heart; you turn about in the other direction, toward eternal life. Repentance is just that simple—turning from the old ways of sin and obeying Jesus.

JESUS SAVES

CONFESSION

4 After we repent, what should be our next step?

Now therefore MAKE CONFESSION unto the Lord God.—Ezra 10:11.

If we CONFESS our sins, he is faithful and just to forgive us our sins, and to cleanse us from all unrighteousness.—1 John 1:9.

We must *confess* our sins. God promises to forgive absolutely *every* sin and to cleanse us from all unrighteousness (wrong doing), through Jesus' blood.

The Junior course was very popular with youth and adults. The course was developed in the 1940s.

The team for the first *Voice of Prophecy* coast-to-coast broadcast in 1942 (*from left*): H. M. S. Richards, speaker; King's Heralds quartet (Bob Seamount, second tenor; Wesley Crane, baritone; George Casebeer, first tenor; Ray Turner, bass); Fordyce Detamore, announcer; and Elmer Digneo, organist.

The 1954 radio team included (*seated*) H. M. S. Richards, speaker, and J. O. Iversen, announcer; (*standing, from left*) Bob Edwards, first tenor; Bob Seamount, second tenor; Del Delker, contralto; Wayne Hooper, baritone; and Jerry Dill, bass.

Bible School staff, circa 1940s. Standing is H. M. J. Richards, father of H. M. S. Richards Sr.

A copy of one of the earlier Bible School diplomas. This is a 1943 diploma belonging to Homer Dever, son-in-law of Fordyce Detamore. Signed by Fordyce Detamore and H. M. S. Richards Sr.

VOP staff with outgoing bags of mail—Bible lessons, letters, and booklets. Circa 1940s.

Bible School Staff, 2006. *Back row left:* Anna Hendargo, Nancy Rieder Kachocki, Denny Kaye, Jan Judd, Gloria Maguire. *Second row left:* Denise Johnson, Miriam Atiga, Lisa Styadi, Helga Hopkins. *Front row left:* Estelita Atiga, Mariel Swenson, Kurt Johnson, Lay Cheng Tan

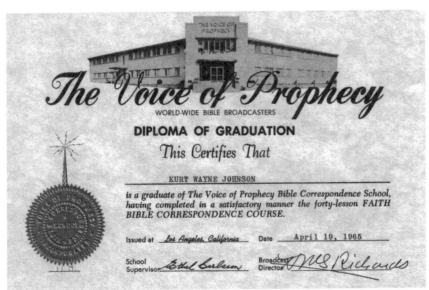

One of the author's personal Bible School graduation diplomas. (See his story beginning on page 47.)